**Also by Cheryl Landon:**

*I Promised My Dad*

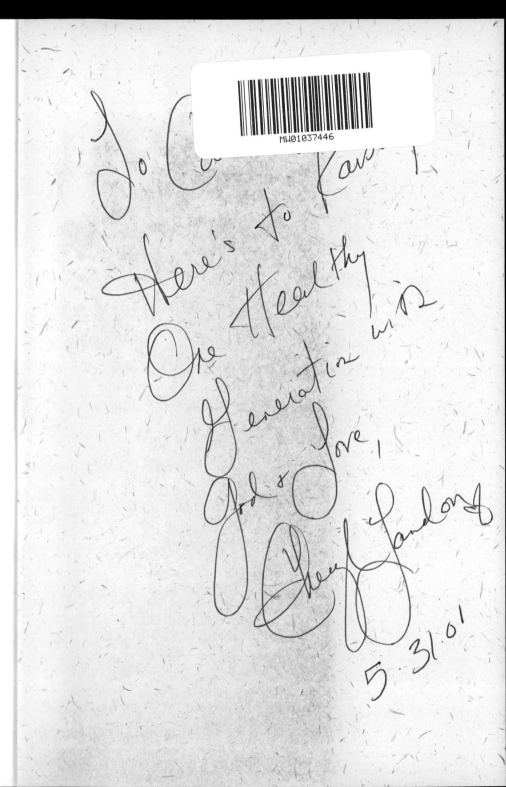

To Co[...]
Here's to Kar[...]
One Healthy
Generation w[...]
God & love,

Cheryl Landon

5·31·01

Micha

*Lege*

# Michael Landon's *Legacy*

*7 Keys to Supercharging Your Life*

## CHERYL LANDON

HAMPTON ROADS

PUBLISHING COMPANY, INC.

for the evolving human spirit

Cover design by Marjoram Productions
Cover art by Corbis Images
Cover photograph by Gary Null, courtesy of NBC

For information write:

Hampton Roads Publishing Company, Inc.
1125 Stoney Ridge Road
Charlottesville, VA 22902

Or call: 804-296-2772
Fax: 804-296-5096
e-mail: hrpc@hrpub.com
Web site: www.hrpub.com

If you are unable to order this book from your local
bookseller, you may order directly from the publisher.
Call 1-800-766-8009, toll-free.

Library of Congress Catalog Card Number: 00-111192

ISBN 1-57174-285-9

10 9 8 7 6 5 4 3 2 1

Printed on acid-free paper in Canada

*To my lord, Jesus Christ,*

and to all Christ-conscious individuals throughout our world, forming one unity devoted to loving one another . . . let us deliberately come together to focus on serving our future generation, "to raise one healthy generation and create an alignment to heal our world!" Together, let us be the voice as "universal born-agains" where individuals are no longer judged as a select few of God's chosen ones. . . . Rather, let us remember how we are all chosen ones rooted in God, our Creator, and let us welcome all races, colors, creeds, religions, and genders as family.

To my beloved dad, to whom I owe my life and further dedicate this book. Like my father, I am here continuing his torch as the "Landon legacy of love and truth" forming the universal paradigm shift, "us" as I promised him.

To my dearest son, James Michael, who gives me greater meaning and purpose to live!

Together, let us sing one universal song to "love one another" with powerful voices, hopeful and strong. Let our children know they are vital to our future, show our youth the way to God, daily practicing the power of love and forgiveness, breaking down all negative barriers—no more prejudices and color lines. Let our youth know they are: "new beginnings" and magnificent! Together, let us deliberately shift our consciousness into taking care of one another . . . Bringing out the best in one another . . . And, yes—we can because we must!

# Acknowledgements

This nine-year journey has been the toughest and most challenging of my life, yet, the most rewarding! And, so I must begin by acknowledging my Lord, Jesus Christ with whom I am reborn.

To my miracle son, James Michael, who inspires me daily.

To my Dad in Heaven who continues to inspire me from above.

To my beloved mother, Lynn.

To Jim, Janice, Shambri and Schyler, Carlos, C-Mar, Mother Mar, a united family; no other can compare.

To Cindy Landon for her unconditional love and devotion to this mission against those who try to tear us apart. There is trust, truth, and Dad's love between us, bonding us forever and always.

To my brothers and sisters, whom I have loved since they were babies, and adore as my dearest siblings.

To other family and friends who also remained by my side through thick and thin: Ginny Jean and Melanie. Kissin Cousins: Bernice and Linda Ann; Dr. Ruby, Marcy, Scott, Barbara, Sharon, Erica, Lizzie, Harry Flinn, Mary Ann, Helen Lacono, S. H. Bruce Merrin and Jo Ann, Ms. Lana, Larry, Scott Brazil, Phyllis, Pam, Holy Holly, St. Paul, Rev. Sue, I love you!

To my biological father, Michael Angelo: I'll love you forever; you'll always be my special Poppa.

To Westlake football team and my adopted sons, you know who you are.

To my ladies at WFWP: Shari, Linda, Kimio, Nora, and Mrs. Sugiyama, all my Japanese and Korean Sisters, and devotedly to Rev. and Dr. Moon;

To my ISP Sister Donzalie Abernathy.

To Pastor Brian and his lovely wife, Laurie, at Gateway Church;

To other special angels, my dearest partner and Christian sister, Janice, with Mo.

To minister-literary agent, Barbara Neighors Deal, who greatly helped me in the preparation of the manuscript.

To Crystal Bush, leading me to my special Hampton Roads Publishing Team, (His Royal Majesty) Frank DeMarco and Bob Friedman, who opened the Heavenly floodgates, renewing my belief and love. Bravo to Hampton Roads, specializing in the vision to spot a bestseller and take it to the ultimate heights so we all can truly "Set the world on fire and inspire!"

To all Michael Landon fans, thank you for your love! I love you all!!!

To all mastery minds and everyday people committed for the betterment of humankind, thank you for your devotion to US. "United Spiritually": New Beginnings . . . for our youth as they so deserve!

"Dad triumphed with wonderful family programs. Let us begin at home with us, our loved ones, and use this power of love to make our world safe for all to prosper. Let us work together to make it happen."

—from my first book, *I Promised My Dad*

# Table of Contents

"Michael would be so proud of his oldest daughter, Cheryl, who has carried the torch for his humanistic beliefs above and beyond the call of daughterly duty. This book is a testament to the love and humanity he exemplified throughout his professional life, and his campaign to bring positive leadership to all who will accept it is alive and well in his daughter's hands. Read it, you'll know what I mean."

—*Harry Flinn,*
*Michael Landon's publicist*
*and dearest friend for twenty years*

# Introduction

In my travels across the nation and Japan—delivering seminars, teaching, coaching, doing radio shows and live shows interacting with millions—I have seen quite clearly that there is great confusion as to who we really are. I have seen how fear runs us, and how many people focus on what is wrong rather than what is right—rather than seeking the best in one another. This patterned behavior and negative belief system are destroying our future generation.

My life has had more than its share of trauma and even tragedy. It has been a very painful, tough journey that continues to this day. But my life's challenges forced me deep into the study of universal laws and life principles, and *the rewards are worth every painful step.*

At times, we all ask, "What is the meaning of life?" and "Really, just what and who is God?" My studies brought me clear, simple answers that anyone can follow.

The universal laws and life principles answering these questions are easy to follow once the concepts are clear, and the results in our daily living truly are miraculous.

My purpose in sharing some extremely personal experiences in a teaching mode is to show how each of us can *immediately* become the miracles we are meant to be. I am doing this to continue to fulfill a promise I made to my dad, so that we may hand down to our future generation a world where dreams do come true; a world filled with hope, unity, and love; a world in which we do truly *"love one another."*

In my Science of Mind studies, I came across an anonymous piece of wisdom that I particularly love. I think that like so much ancient wisdom, it becomes more accessible when rephrased into modern language. Here is my rendering of it. I hope it speaks to you as it does to me.

## A Miracle for Us

The miracle enables us to see our brothers and sisters without their pasts, and so perceive them as born again. The errors are all past, and by perceiving one another without these errors, we are releasing them. And since their past is ours, we share in this release. Let no dark cloud out of our past obscure them, for truth lies only in the present, and we will find it if we seek it there. We have looked for it where it is not, and therefore have not found it. Learn, then, to seek it where it is, and it will dawn on eyes that see. Our past was made in anger—these were errors of our thinking—and if we use it to attack the present, we will not see the freedom that the present holds. We will miss the miracles in action available to us every second of every moment in every day!

# Part One:
# The Promise

# 1

It is late at night, in May, 1973. It is in the middle of the desolate Arizona desert, and very, very dark. No houses, no lights on this desert highway, except for a run-down shack where there has just been a party. There's been a lot of celebration. Kids have been drinking; they've been smoking pot. There's lots of laughter coming from this shack, but it's time the party is ended. Time to get on the bus and return to the campus, a two-hour drive away.

But four people do not get on the bus. Instead, they get into a little navy blue Volkswagen bug, making a choice. One of the four is a nineteen-year-old college girl. She gets into the front seat next to the driver, a blind date, someone she had never met before. He starts to drive onto the highway, turning left. But the bus is turning right. The guy is so drunk, he is going in the wrong direction, toward Mexico.

The girl in the passenger seat says, "You're going the wrong way. You've got to go right and follow the bus." He is laughing, thinking it is all hysterical. And he pops the clutch and stalls the engine, and all the lights go off, and they are stuck there in the middle of the highway, and suddenly there is a big Buick coming eighty miles an hour straight toward them.

It hits them so hard, the impact sounds like a bomb. The VW Beetle flies the length of a football field, somersaulting three times forward, twice sideways; crushing bodies; screams filling the air.

Hearing that terrible noise, the bus driver stops, and he and the passengers see the VW bug lying smashed flat, except for one section.

Meanwhile the girl in the passenger seat sees the guy in the back seat hitting the glass of the car window so hard that it cuts his head off. She sees her girlfriend hit the glass so hard that it cuts her head literally in half as she is flying in and out of the back window.

The driver is crushed by the steel pressing on him. It breaks all of his bones, and his blood is pouring out all over. He lands on top of her, and she hits the windshield so hard she breaks the glass, breaks her neck, cracks open her forehead, ruptures organs. She has punctured her spleen, punctured her lung, and broken her ribs—and she is trapped in the passenger side, with the body of the driver on top of her and blood pouring down.

And she's bleeding to death.

There are no more screams. There is dead silence.

The bus doesn't come near them. No one gets off the bus, because they are sure that no one could have survived that crash. But the bus driver calls ahead and asks for the paramedics, and the paramedics eventually arrive. The girl has been trapped inside this car in the darkness, with this dead body on top of her. She is frightened. Terrified. And when the paramedics and the police look at this car—so badly flattened, except for this little area that remains intact—they say "surely no one could survive in that." They have to tear the door off, and when the door is off, they see the dead bodies, an awful, grotesque sight.

As they remove the driver, they realize that the girl is alive, but they can't recognize her. Her forehead is split wide open, and she's a bloody mess. But she starts fighting like a wild animal, fighting for her life, reaching out and fighting and grabbing and tearing and kicking. And because she is doing that, she's saving her life. One lung has collapsed, and her fighting is keeping her other lung operating.

They put her onto a gurney, and put her into the back of the ambulance and begin emergency procedures. She sees her girlfriend lifted out and put onto another gurney next to her. The two men are dead. And the ambulance goes rushing off and her girlfriend dies in the ambulance, but she doesn't know it because the paramedics are working on her, stitching her head up, without anesthetic. No anesthetic can be used because she has a concussion.

She has four blood transfusions while she's in the ambulance. They administer blood, they stitch up her head, and they phone ahead to the hospital, in Tucson, Arizona.

The hospital has no idea who she is, because she isn't carrying any ID on her. The doctor on call is from India, Dr. Rashid Khan. She hears him say, "I believe this could be a very pretty woman," and he tells them he knows that no anesthetic can be used.

She's still fighting everybody. She is using all her will, all her strength, fist-fighting as if truly fighting for her life. Two male nurses hold her shoulders down, and two hold her feet down, and they begin cutting off her long sweater coat. It is all full of blood, blood all over it.

When they finally get the jacket off, they have to make a cut into her chest—with no anesthetic—so that they can insert a tube and reinflate her collapsed lung. It's so painful, she screams, and falls into a coma. It is beyond what she could tolerate.

However she does have time enough to tell them that she is Michael Landon's daughter.


2


It's the middle of the night, and Michael Landon is doing a show in Salt Lake City. He and his wife, Lynn, take a phone call in their hotel room, and he hears the doctor on the other end say, "Your daughter has been in a very serious car accident. She is the only survivor. Quick. We need you to get over here."

They charter a flight to Tucson, and they get to the hospital. But before they see their daughter, the doctor pulls them aside and says, "I didn't want to tell you this over the phone, but your daughter is dying. She will not make it through the night. It will take a miracle."

Then Michael goes into the Intensive Care Unit and sees his daughter. He later said there were tubes coming out of every opening that you could imagine. He breaks down and starts crying. And something inside of him—a higher force, whatever you want to call this connection—tells him to talk to her. And so he touches her hand, and he starts as best he can. He starts telling her, "Fight, baby, fight. Fight, baby, fight." He's chanting the words. "Fight, baby, fight." As he's saying this, every repetition gets stronger and stronger. He's in focus, focused only on her, looking at her and telling her, "Fight, baby, fight. Don't give up. We love you. It's too soon for you to go." And he keeps talking to her.

The nurse comes up and says, "Why are you talking to her? She can't hear you. She's in a coma. You're wasting your time." But he won't listen to the nurse. He continues to talk to his daughter. He remains by his daughter's side for three days and three nights. And—although it will be many years before he ever publicly speaks of it—he makes a promise to God. He won't give up; he remains, talking to her.

After three days, she comes out of the coma, and she sees her dad at the foot of her bed. And what's so unusual is that she needs to have corrective lenses because she's legally blind, but at that moment she sees her dad perfectly clearly, from five feet away. And then the pain hits her. And oh my God!

Up until this time, she has been in another place, experiencing a warmth, experiencing other entities, and having a conversation. She was in another world. It was very clear that she was with Jesus. Very clear that she was talking to Jesus, and being told very specifically what she needed to do with her life. And that there were messages and information given to her that she had to return to teach. But she came back not knowing what had happened. She came back to that pain, that incredible pain, and remembered nothing from before the crash until much later when she went through hypnosis. When she woke up, it was like a new entity in a body, losing a lot of the memory, the old person, the old memory. Over time, it became very clear that by the time she came out of the coma, her whole personality had changed drastically. She was not the same person.

3

I was that nineteen-year-old girl.

They had stitched up my head. They had reinflated my lung. While I was in a coma, there was nothing more they could do. They were just trying to be sure that I stayed alive. And it was three days before they could give me any pain relief, because of the concussion.

They were putting a tube down my throat into my stomach to bring up this green junk—bile—because of the spleen, which was rupturing, though it hadn't ruptured yet. I hadn't had medication. I was crying. I was in so much pain. "Please give me some medicine. Please. Oh my God. I can't take this pain." And I remember my mom crying over me. She was helpless because they couldn't give me any medicine till the concussion had eased.

And I was dying of agony. They put the tube down me, and here's this guy next to me who had gotten shot. The nurses couldn't control him. He was screaming and yelling and kicking pans and stuff. And I remember saying to him—with the tube down my throat—"Would you please shut up. I've had to listen to you all night long. And I need to get some sleep too." And the guy shut up. The nurses came in and said, "Thank you so much."

Then on the third day, the doctor came in and saw me and he was able to give me pain relief. He said, "We almost lost you."

I was taken up to a room. And all of the sudden I had the most unbelievable horrible pain in my stomach. I thought, "Oh, if only I could go to the bathroom." I was thinking I was constipated. So I got up out of bed on my own, and I went into the bathroom. I looked into the mirror and I didn't know who that person was. I didn't recognize who it was at all. It scared me.

I sat on the toilet, and then I felt I was going to pass out. I screamed for help. A cleaning lady happened to be nearby, and she came in just in time. I fainted, falling forward, but she caught me before I hit the floor. She saved my life. If I had fallen down and cracked my head open again, my body could not have taken that.

So I was being taken down to ICU again. I remember looking at the doctor, and he said, "Your spleen has ruptured. We've got to take you into surgery." I looked at him and I said, "Am I going to die now?" And he said, "I will do everything I can to save you."

4

Michael Landon was Jewish, but he didn't go to a synagogue regularly. He didn't practice a particular religion. He was just a good man. But at this moment, in this hospital, he reached out for God, because that was the only place he could go to, to pray for a miracle. And he made God a promise in return for his daughter's life.

I learned about it only in May, 1991, a few short weeks before Dad made his own transition. It was an article in *Life* magazine:

The most important promise I ever made, was a promise to God and I made it while holding the hand of my daughter Cheryl, who was lying near death in a hospital in Tucson. She'd been in a terrible automobile accident and her body was shattered. She was in a deep coma, and the doctors gave her no chance at all. But I wouldn't, I couldn't give up.

So I stayed with her in intensive care. Day after day, holding her hand, talking to her, telling her that I loved her, that we all loved her. The nurses said it was useless, that she couldn't hear me. But I didn't listen.

When Cheryl finally woke up, she told me things I'd said to her. And I spoke to God. I promised God that if he would let her live, I would do something useful with my life, something to make the world a little better because I'd been there.

Cheryl lived and I've tried to keep that promise ever since.

He had never talked to me about his reaction to my automobile crash, and had never mentioned his promise.

"Since that day," Dad wrote, "every script I've written and every series I've produced—not only *Little House on the Prairie* and *Highway to Heaven*, but the ones that didn't make it and the one I've just started—have expressed the things I most deeply believe. I believe in God, I believe in family, I believe in truth between people,

I believe in the power of love. I believe that we really are created in God's image, that there is God in all of us."

5

At the time of the crash, my values were in the material world, and I wasn't at all self-reflective about it. I was very privileged. At the same time, I loved people, I cared for people, and I always knew that I was going to be a teacher. I just hadn't put it all together.

While I was in the coma, I was in another world for a while. I know that I was with Jesus. I don't say much about that time, but that was when I learned that the path I had been following was not my destiny. I got messages about my future life, though it would be a long time before I would remember any of this.

But from the other world, I began to hear "fight, baby, fight." It was Dad. And that gradually pulled me out of that world. I regained consciousness and saw Dad, sitting at the end of the bed, holding my foot and looking at me. I was shocked that I could see his features so clearly, since I am so very nearsighted. I thought for a moment I must have had my contact lenses in. They weren't. They'd been removed in the emergency room. Yet I saw Dad's face sharply defined, even though he was more than five feet away. I remember thinking, "Wow, this is like a miracle. I can see without my glasses or lenses." But then came an intense ache that ran the length of my body, and grew in intensity and was soon a constant excruciating pain. I asked him what had happened, and then my mother came back into the room, and they gently put their hands on me. We were all crying.

If he hadn't been there calling me, I don't think I could have come back. He loved me so unconditionally that it was like returning to safety, returning to someone who loved me. I knew I belonged with him. Had he not been there, I might not have had anything to come back to. Without him, there wasn't enough to come back to.

He saved me by his love, by his determination not to let me go. And that was the second time he'd done it.

## 6

I had had a very rough beginning to my childhood. My mother left my biological father and me, in order to pursue her modeling career, when I was two years old. For seven years, I grew up living with my father's relatives, thinking that I was a mistake, that I should not have been born. I really felt unloved. I was the youngest, and I didn't have the nurturing love of my mother, or the protection of my father. A couple of my cousins were being abused, and they took it out on me because I was the youngest.

As a child, I was beaten up almost every day. I was beaten up, and slapped in the face so much. I remember being stuck into a bathtub with blood pouring down. It was an Italian family, and the hot temper of the Italian sometimes comes out as a slap across the face and yelling. And so I was at the butt end. I had built a little hiding place in an empty field. And I had dug a hole and I would hide in it. It was the only protection that I had. There was no one I could go to.

I first met Michael Landon when I was seven years old, living with my grandparents, and he started dating my mother. I didn't know he was a celebrity. In fact, he wasn't a celebrity at the time; he was just in the beginning of *Bonanza*. But it was like I recognized him right away and he recognized me. There was this tremendous bond there. And he saved me. He knew I was a very depressed little girl, starved for affection. He instantly knew I was in bad hands, because he had grown up in the same situation.

His mother was a psychotic schizophrenic. He never knew if she was going to be attempting suicide in front of him that day or if she was going to try to kill him. And she did both of those. Often. His mother would wait for him to come home to stick her head in the oven. Dad used to say that for the longest time he didn't know that the oven was for baking food, rather than sticking your head in. He would cry and beg his mother, "Please don't kill yourself." He said he would be vomiting from being so upset, and she would be singing some happy song. On his fifth birthday, she told him, "You're not cute any more; I don't love you." His father never stood up for him.

There is no way a new soul could come into this world and endure what he endured—and not only from his mother. He experienced prejudice growing up in an anti-Semitic neighborhood in Collingswood, New Jersey, and again when he won an athletic scholarship to USC. The football players hated him because he was a scrawny Jew with long hair. They held him down, shaved off his hair, put hot balm on his private area, and chained him to a sink. And he lost his ability to throw the javelin, which was the basis for his scholarship.

He had no money, no family, nowhere to go. He went through one trial after another: rejection, betrayal, not having any security, sometimes not having a roof over his head, sleeping on porches, selling blankets, selling books door to door, working in a ribbon factory. But there was a power in him. I believe that God used Dad to inspire us. I do believe that my dad was a prophet, a true prophet, because he took all of these experiences and taught us the power of love. He was an advanced soul in this world with a purpose.

He didn't allow these experiences to make him bitter. Instead he developed a phenomenal sense of humor, and an unbelievable wit. And he gave me what nobody was able to give him when he was a child. He gave me unconditional acceptance and unconditional love. And he gave me protection. I found out years later that he got my biological father to release me into his custody by threatening to sue him, because he knew I was being abused. So I got to live with him and my mother.

## 7

Michael Landon and my mother were so in love. I have never seen a love like their love. Their love was inspirational. And love cured him. Before he married my mother, he had gotten into pill popping and sedatives. But my mother inspired him and protected him. She enabled him to build his empire. She was there in all the hard days, the hard times. She was his angel.

From that love with my mother came this incredible connection between him and me. I refer to him as my dad, and he referred to me as his daughter. And his unconditional love saved me during times when I couldn't believe in myself, when I felt so unworthy.

You have to have been in that situation to understand. People who are secure in love do not understand what it feels like not to feel good enough. I couldn't feel confidence because I thought I was a mistake. I was not supposed to have been born. My mother had me when she was twenty years old, and then she split. She told me later on in my life, "I didn't want to be a mother. I wanted to go on and model and have fun." And I was stuck in this hell, being beaten up, feeling that my mother didn't want me. But Michael Landon loved me as no one had ever loved me. He loved me when I couldn't love myself.

I was his daughter for thirty years, and I am the only one of all the family members who spent that much time with him, in all phases of his life. I knew him from the time I was seven years old until he died on July 1, 1991. My brothers and sisters are nine, twelve, eighteen, and twenty-one years younger, so there's a vast difference in experience.

The other times that I felt Dad's unconditional love were in dealing with my biological father, who was so jealous of Dad Landon that he would verbally abuse me. I didn't live with this man and he didn't do anything to be my dad, and my memories of him were bad. Yet he would say, "How dare you love Michael Landon? You have to pick between him or me. Don't you ever call him Dad. I'm your dad."

Michael Landon wanted to adopt me, but my biological father wouldn't allow it. Michael would always say, "Cheryl, don't worry about a name change. You will always be my daughter, and name doesn't mean anything."

When I was dating and I was feeling rejected, or the guy was dating somebody else, I would go to my father and cry. I wouldn't go to my mother. She didn't get it. But Dad would help me. And the times that I felt so lost in my life, Dad cried with me. He said, "Don't you think I ever feel lost? I feel lost too, and I'm an adult." He was always available for me to talk to. He was very easy to be around.

When I was a little girl and I couldn't fall asleep at night, he sang *Puff the Magic Dragon* to me. He hugged me. He always brushed my hair. He called me his beauty. He made me feel like I was a woman, a girl—a female of character, of purpose—who was so loved by him that I was able to get through that darkness. Even the time I tried to commit suicide.

## 8

It was two years after the night of the crash.

I had been in a psychiatric hospital, and had had to fake my way out, because all they did was shoot you up with Thorazine and sit you in front of the psychiatrist. I hated the place. They allowed smoking and there was no fresh air. You didn't deal with feelings. I hated it, so I faked being healthy. And about a year later, I was doing every drug I could get my hands on, because I couldn't face reality. I hated reality. I hated it! God had made a mistake.

Plus, I was still in physical pain, and having nightmares. I couldn't sleep because all I could see was the car accident going on, over and over and over and over and over. Watching my friend getting his head chopped off.

I was nineteen at the car crash. And I was so angry at God, because first I had gone through all this pain and then I was told that I was going to be a cripple in a wheelchair. I wanted to get married and have babies, and that was not going to happen. I wanted to teach and I couldn't. All my dreams were smashed. So I went into a deep, dark depression. And it wasn't because of the drugs. It was just that God made a mistake.

I kept wondering, "Why did I survive? I shouldn't have survived. They were better than me. They should have lived and I should have died." Today people talk about survivor guilt, and apparently survivor guilt is a very normal thing, but nobody explained it to me, and I didn't understand it.

So it brought up my childhood issues. Why was I alive? Why was I even born? My mother didn't want me. And God?

People say that when you go through a near-death experience it's all lovey-dovey and wonderful. Well, mine wasn't. I didn't have this euphoric experience. I was so caught up in, "What the heck is it with God? What if there is no God? If there's a God, then he's a prejudiced God. He's a selective God. Only certain people get to benefit, and I'm not one of them. He isn't fair." All I could think of was that I must have been born under the wrong sign. I was doomed. I was born to suffer.

I was full of what my dad termed emotional darkness: bitterness, pain, guilt. Why did God save me? I was really angry at Him. If I had understood that this was a normal feeling, and that I had the power to change my choices at any moment, that I had a connection with God right then and there, that I chose my state and my feelings, that I was in control of that to begin with, perhaps I would not have gotten so far down into that darkness.

But I never thought, and no one ever told me, that I had the ability to *choose* my reaction to the pain, or to the guilt or any of that. It just wasn't a concept to me. My mother's belief system was that you married wealthy and the man took care of you. And at this time—at the time of my accident and the years that followed—she didn't get it. She was being taken care of very well by my dad. She never lacked anything. She had yet to experience this kind of emotional pain. So I had no role model; nobody had ever talked about the idea that we have a choice about how we react to whatever happens to us.

9

I was at my maternal grandparents' house. I tried to run through a plate glass window to cut myself up, and my uncle, Bob Noe, stopped me. He came rushing and grabbed me and threw me on the floor and sat on top of me, crying. And once again, Dad came to my rescue. He came into the bedroom of my grandparents' house. Didn't say a word. He sat down and he reached his arms up and out for me to come to him. And I went to him and I sat on his lap and he held me. And we both started crying. And he told me how much he loved me. He said, "You're an addict, and I won't watch you die."

I didn't know at the time that he had been addicted to pills. But he knew that feeling of unworthiness, that feeling of confusion. He shared with me that he had been there and that he knew what I was going through. But, he said, it was up to me to make that final choice. Either I could commit to spend at least ten months at this place called CEDU, or I could go to jail. Either way, he wanted me to know that he was not going to put up with it any more, because he could not stand to watch me die. Tragedies affect people differently. I descended into darkness. My dad ascended to the spiritual value of witnessing God firsthand. He wrote the series of *Little House on the Prairie* episodes about Mary going blind directly from my experience.

After I began treatment at CEDU, I began to unravel the darkness and the light started coming in. Higher wisdom started coming into play. I had to release the darkness, the pain, the bitterness, the hatred. And once I got through the hatred I realized I was not the same person at all that I had been before the car crash.

21

## 10

It's spelled C-E-D-U, but inside the program we say that CEDU means "see" yourself as you are and "do" something about it. Mel and Brigetta Wasserman founded it in the seventies, up in the San Bernadino Mountains, and their children Mark and Danna continue the work now. Their motto is "The Truth Will Set You Free." In practice, that means taking personal responsibility for who you are, getting to know who you are as an individual.

In other words, Cheryl wasn't Cheryl Pontrelli or Cheryl Landon, but Cheryl. Who was Cheryl? I had never really gotten to know myself, because my mother had always told me to dress a certain way and behave a certain way. She brought me up to be a lady, which I love. And my dad gave me unconditional love, and was always there for me. But I never knew who *Cheryl* was. I mean, I was Cheryl Michael-Landon's-Daughter. I had a lot of people jealous and teasing me, because it was a privileged life. But on the other hand I was Cheryl Michael-Landon's-Daughter, not Cheryl On-Her-Own.

CEDU was the best move I could have made. They took away my Mercedes. They took away all my own clothes. I wasn't allowed to even pluck my eyebrows, much less wear makeup. I couldn't wear my contact lenses instead of glasses. I couldn't hide behind the things that made up my appearance. And that was the best thing, because I was so dependent on looks, and the social graces, and all that. At CEDU, they strip you down to owning who you are.

Partly they do it through peer pressure. There's nothing more powerful than having your own peers bust you from your beliefs in lies, in what you hide behind. And that's what we did to each other.

And then we all had jobs, and they were always putting us in a position where we were in fear. Not in fear for our lives, of course, but being constantly forced out of our comfort zone. For instance, phone solicitations was one job. I had to dial for dollars and I was terrified to ask people for money. Then they had the humiliating jobs in the very beginning where I bussed tables, cleaned dishes, served people their dinners. Not everybody would find it humiliating to serve others, I know. But I was a princess. I was used to having servants. I went from princess to pauper.

After a while I moved up to being the baker, and I baked for 150 people.

But according to my belief system at the time, you had only princesses and paupers, so if you weren't one, you must be the other. And when I went through that, I realized that Dad had made me a princess. I wasn't a princess of my own accord. I was a princess because of Michael Landon meeting my every need, including my emotional needs; which means that I was dependent on him. And I still see that to this day. I can see how much of my significance is still attached to him. And that's the key here: What do we attach our significance to?

Before CEDU, I attached my significance to this royalty of being in a mansion, and being served, and marrying a rich man. And that is where a lot of people get caught up, to where they are not being who they are. It's not okay to be who you are. So now we get to: Who are you? Who was I? Who was Cheryl?

At CEDU, if you were a minute late to work, you had to wear this mechanic's one-piece suit, and they chopped all my hair off and I had to clean toilets and all that stuff. I had had hair down to my waist. It was all cut off. It was humiliating, because I depended on my hair, like I depended on my dad. It was the story of Samson all over again. It has always been a part of me. I like having long hair. (Today some people say "you're too old for long hair" and I don't care.) That was a big change.

I knew that I had ten months to get it together, or I'd wind up in jail. That was what my dad said. I had made a ten-month commitment, and if I broke that ten-month commitment, I would go to jail. He would not let me back into the house. So I knew I was in there for ten months. I really didn't have a choice. But as it turned out, I loved it, because it was truth.

You know, truth doesn't come necessarily in words. It's a hunch. It's an instinct. You just know it. You know when someone's telling you truth. You know if someone is a phony. I know there are cons out there. There are great manipulators. But you know it, just as a child senses someone who's not nice, just as an animal senses it.

## 11

There were about 250 students and teachers altogether; mostly kids who came from group homes and foster homes and juvenile homes. And there were a handful of private students like me.

The philosophy at CEDU is to give people the opportunity to be grounded in *who they are*. Which, of course, involves knowing who we are. It is "Who I am" as opposed to, "Who am I?" ("Who am I?" is always outside the individual. It is always searching for love *outside*, looking for an answer outside of yourself, versus being grounded in who you are.) They would put us through a series of talk sessions, lasting sometimes even twenty-four or forty-eight hours. They call those sessions "pro-feeds," playing off *The Prophet* by Kahlil Gibran. CEDU brought anthroposophy, the spiritual science of man, into the classroom. They also used self-actualization—the work of psychologist Abraham Maslow. Altogether it was an eclectic group of self-actualization experiences.

At the same time, the rules were very strict. We weren't allowed to have sex. We weren't allowed to date.

Everything was very controlled. Because if we dated, and had sex, then we'd be depending on that person to make us feel good. They wanted us to experience our full potential.

Academic classes were taught through the philosophy of Emerson College, in England. We studied arts and crafts, English, the basic academic curriculum, but with the anthroposophic flair for connecting us to that particular subject matter. For example, when we were studying the French Revolution, they would break us into groups and say, "you're the paupers, you're the king and queen, you're the lords. Now, you're not having any food, but you're having everything that you want." And so they would create this situation. Instead of telling us what happened, we had to come up with what we were going to do.

The paupers and the regular everyday people decided to revolt. The kings and queens wanted the barons and the lords to deal with it. The lesson set up the dynamics of what really happened. And this way we learned, because we had to go within and challenge ourselves to come up with the answers. It tied into real life: "How would I feel if I were in that situation?"

And that moved into the dynamics of the contemporary lifestyle today, how we are dependent on our parents to make our lives work. How we're dependent on a boyfriend or a girlfriend to get us to feel acceptable because they like us. Or we're dependent on money.

Money is security. So a lot of people act without integrity; they manipulate, lie, or steal.

Not that they drew these conclusions for us. They helped us to draw them, mostly by group discussions. It's very powerful.

## 12

But I was still having nightmares. I was depressed. I had come to hate God. Psychiatry hadn't helped. I had been ready to kill myself. I went to CEDU only as a last resort. But something happened there that was very profound.

My feelings had been telling me that I should relive the car accident, but I didn't trust myself. I was scared to death. I had been told before, by my psychiatrist, to do everything I could *not* to relive it. The psychiatric hospital even took all the pictures and threw them away. But I was still having nightmares, and I was actually blocking the higher person, the advanced soul, that I had experienced. I stopped it coming back to me.

So one day, Mel Wasserman had me go back, using self-hypnosis, and reexperience my car accident for the first time, moment by moment, in such detail that I experienced everything. And it was then, for the first time, that I cried. My mom and my dad and society disapproved of crying. You were supposed to tough it out and move on, so I had not been allowed to cry over my accident. But that was what I needed. I needed to experience those emotions so I could let the dead die and be buried. When we don't allow a situation in our life to be buried, we cannot move on with our growth as a person.

Mel and I went into this room in the morning and I relived the whole thing. So much came out that I had suppressed! I cried and cried and screamed. Finally it was afternoon, and Mel said, "I want you to take some time and be by yourself and go out into the forest," and it was there, for the first time, that I thanked God for saving me. It was the first time that I realized it wasn't God who put me in that car, but it was my own choice. After that day, after the walk in the forest, the nightmares stopped. I gave myself to Jesus Christ and became born again.

I'll always remember that day. That day, it was Mel and Jesus Christ who saved me.

## 13

That time, Dad *couldn't* save me, because in this area he was crippled too. He felt that you couldn't allow yourself to cry. You had to be tough. It wasn't safe otherwise. And in fact, I think that was one reason why my dad contracted cancer. He always had to be tough, but there were some issues that he needed to cry about, that he needed to express, and he didn't.

Fortunately, he had found find my mom's nurturing love. That love carried him during the years that led to his becoming a mega-celebrity. And I don't think she was ever given fair credit for that. *Highway to Heaven* was her idea, for instance. But he didn't have anybody to be a father to him. Or a mother. He never did experience either a mother's love or a father's.

He could cry very easily on demand, when he was acting, but he didn't express his private emotions. They scared him too much. Suppressing our feelings results in these pent-up, locked-up emotions that express in bizarre behaviors. We have to express—we need a place to cry, to express our feelings. We all do.

Maybe one reason that I was able to go beyond where he could go, in dealing with emotions, was that he had given me the secure base that he had never had himself. He gave me a world of love that I am always grateful for. I feel very privileged. So here is where we grow, generation by generation, because that's what love is about. What lets us live on is how we set up the next generation. If we don't empower our future generation, we will self-destruct.

## 14

I stayed there for two years. The first year was as a student, and the second year as a teacher. When I graduated from CEDU, I did not have an easy time achieving anything, but I learned that I would be okay as long as I knew truth and I stuck with truth. The truth was that I was a woman with a tremendous amount of talent and potential and intelligence, and that I do have a mission—and that no man can make me a whole person, nor can a job.

After I graduated the course at CEDU, I came back for a second year as a counselor and teacher. During all that time, I saw my parents only when I got to go home on weekends and holidays. This was the first time I'd ever really been away from them, except for my time at the University of Arizona. At the end of the two years, I needed to move on. My mother has this rule that once you leave home, you're never allowed back, so I moved to San Francisco, where my uncle Bob lived. Bob, my mother's younger brother, the man who saved me when I tried to kill myself, was vice president of First American Title Company. I went to work for him. And I worked very well for the company, but something was so *missing*.

Then one day I was visiting Dad and he said, "Let's go for a drive," and I went for a drive with him, and he said, "What's going on with you? How are you feeling?"

I said, "Dad, I miss teaching so much. I really know I'm meant to be a teacher."

He said, "You know, I always felt that about you."

He had started me writing as a young girl. I loved psychodrama and I loved working with kids, especially after CEDU, helping them realize who they are. So he said he would pay my way through graduate school, and he did.

I got a master's degree in education from the college of Notre Dame—not the one in Indiana, but a spin-off coed school in San Francisco that's run by nuns. I had learned of Emerson College in England at CEDU, and so I went there and learned of the work of Ralph Waldo Emerson and Rudolph Steiner.

I think once you study Steiner and Emerson, it's like riding a bicycle, it never leaves you. It's very powerful. Emerson's work is pure. He reminds us that we need to get back into nature, to return to the basic fact that we are all connected. When we start living separately, we allow ourselves to be tempted into manipulation, jealousy, envy—things that keep us separate from one another. But when we connect with nature, we're all one. We're of all the same source. And when we realize that we're all of the same source, we don't want to hurt other people. We don't want to cheat and lie and betray. We get along. We rely on each of us taking care of one another. This is the opposite of not caring about others, and being willing to hurt them. He reminds me of Emmet Fox.

Emerson and Fox were men of the 1800s, so we're not talking about New Age. Today, if you say New Age, many people think it's weird and that you're of Satan. But the 1800s was the time of the New Thought movement, and there is nothing unspiritual about New Thought thinkers: Emmet Fox and Emerson and even Thoreau, William James, and Holmes belong with these people. To me, they are centered in Jesus, and I believe Jesus is the most profound teacher. Their teaching was all based on love and getting along and cooperation with nature, cooperation with one another. And that, to me, is the key to the preservation of society.

Rudolph Steiner got us into curative education. That is, education has to come from within, and that's the bottom line. I don't care what field you're in or who you are, it all has to come from within. Steiner is about going within instead of going outside. It's about stripping us down to our personal truths. Steiner's educational message is that we learn something not by memorizing facts but by *experiencing* the facts. That's the natural way for us to learn. It stays with you forever that way.

Their way of teaching is like virtual reality. You are involved in the middle of the experience rather than being forced to memorize, which will leave you stuck in your head. When you get the experience inside you, you're experiencing it on all levels—the soul, the heart, the mind—and that's what makes us tick. We're not just automatons that can be told to feel this and do this or feel that.

You are your own person. You can look at a tree and you know that tree isn't just what you're seeing from the one perspective. You can see the tree from all perspectives and you know that it's from the earth and grows up and forms its branches. How many times do you look at a tree? People don't bother to look at the branches, at the way that it flows, at the many limbs involved; or think that there are roots underneath, or that an oak tree comes from a little acorn. And, so it gets you thinking more, and you train your mind to realize that there is more than just this one flat facet without dimensions.

And it's the same with people. You stop looking at them as flat, without dimensions. You learn to make connections, that we're all connected. That's the theory of all of those naturalists. They don't say all this explicitly, but this is what I have picked up from studying it, and I've been studying it for twenty-seven years—so far.

## 15

Michael Landon built everybody up. He worked hard. He gave us the most perfect fantasy world. He deserved to be happy. But he wasn't getting happiness at home. After Dad's very public, very horrible divorce from my mother, she shared with us kids some letters that he had written to her. In one of those letters, he said that his life was becoming so gray. He said, "To work as hard as I do, and not to get anything from it is depressing." And he said the same thing to me—that he just wasn't happy. What had happened?

Back in the beginning, when we lived in Encino, we would sit in the carport on hot days when the air conditioner broke down. We would pull out the card table, and we would eat this delicious salad he'd make. We had just the everyday wonderful routine, and my mother was happy in those carport days. But then we lost the essence.

I watched my father grow from loving and from building his own home, and planting, and planning his grass, roses, and building little forts in the back. He just loved to be part of building something. And then, when it all came, he got bored. So he got himself into another environment. The next environment was Beverly Hills, and the mansion and the maids and the butlers, and the fancier cars, and with that came more problems.

Now, he was watching my mother becoming increasingly obsessed with money, and affecting an air of royalty. It had gotten to the point that she would ring a silver bell for servants to serve her meal. That was not my dad. My dad couldn't stand it. Mom and Dad had gone in different directions.

First it was a maid. And then it was a maid and a butler, and then another maid, and then Mom was being served breakfast in bed every day. She totally got into being a princess, and that wasn't Dad's thing. Of course, the responsibility for that was his. He said himself, "I made your mother into who she became." He used to call her an aristocrat, and say he was a blue-collar person, and finally they had nothing in common but the kids. And of course, as they say, it takes two to tango. They shared the responsibility.

I do believe that he enjoyed some of that Beverly Hills lifestyle. Our Christmases were always phenomenal. Our family holidays were phenomenal. But things did change. The dynamics changed—the dynamics of the now ultra-mega celebrity. Now, he couldn't go out without people invading his privacy. His life was now lived in the celebrity fishbowl. Even when we went out to dinner, he was always having people hounding him and interrupting dinner, or pulling on his clothes. When Dad was on tour, the girls would always tear at him.

In fact, when *Bonanza* was really strong, Lorne and Nancy Greene and us, we would all be in the same hotel, and Mom and I would be told to go with Lorne and Nancy, and they would keep Dad separate, because the fans had this respect for Lorne. They would say, "Hello, Mr. Cartwright," and show him the greatest respect. And then, same hotel, same exit, they would paw at Little Joe.

So anyway, we had had fourteen years of having people interrupting us during dinner, and constantly invading our privacy. The tabloids would be outside the house with their cameras. They would want to know all the scoop. There was no privacy anymore. And then it became a question: With the maids inside the house, who was going to sell the story?

And as to home life? My father, at that point, got up at four in the morning, came home at dinnertime, ate his dinner with the family, played with the kids and us upstairs, and went to bed. On the weekends, we always were together, always in some competitive sport like tennis, or having friends and families over. But we didn't go out, because we were under the spotlight and he was a private man.

## 16

Dad was always into work. Work took his mind off his personal life. And it was also fun. He loved it. My father did everything in television. He is the only man in television history to successfully wear four hats. He was writer, editor, producer, director, and actor. (Five hats, but they don't count editor.) Dad did everything from the writing to scouting location, so he was just consumed with the work.

With it all came stifling expectations on him to be the best, to produce the best shows, to keep up the viewership. Those were his own expectations, but they also came from the networks. And he had a huge mansion and all these cars and all this staff, so he was expected to perform at a certain level.

We didn't have those particular expectations laid on us. But my mother had expectations: "This is how you act. This is how you dress. And you have to marry a rich man." Those are all very heavy expectations, not about producing wealth, but about consuming wealth. And it's crippling to have so much money and not have the tools that the everyday person has, the confidence to go out and get a job. I see that in my old friends whom I don't relate to at all now. They're so depressed. I think, "You're in a $4.7 million mansion with three of the most expensive cars that you can imagine, and you're going on one-month trips and you're depressed?" But of course you're depressed if you're looking for satisfaction where it can't be found. If I ever again have lots of money, I will have protection from the same disadvantages and problems and really serious disabilities of wealth as long as I remember to stay grounded in God, and stay grounded in who I am. That's something that people can do at all income levels, which makes it a universal answer.

Michael Landon knew who he was. He knew he was a creative individual. He was a success—and still had the weight of all that on him. I think he would have been happier if all that money hadn't come to him. He wanted to return to a simple way of life. But he didn't know how. How can you return to a simple way of life if you're a celebrity and you can't even go out to a restaurant? His trips became limited to certain resorts. So all that money and celebrity status did restrict. That's life in the celebrity fishbowl.

He had been so happy in Encino, but he couldn't continue to live there when he became a mega-celebrity. The people who think that having money and being a celebrity is ultimate happiness are not prepared for the truth. The truth is, you lose all your privacy. The expectations on you are even greater and more demanding. You have networks to answer to. You have to keep up a high level of performance. You have to be "on" all the time, to be the best, to be the most popular. This is true of any mega-celebrity.

So Dad was at a crossroads in his life, and Cindy came along and nurtured his playful side. I don't believe that it was a midlife crisis. Dad and Cindy met on the set, just like my mother had met my dad on the set all those years ago. And they were playing and having fun, the way he and my mother used to.

17

Now, in talking about divorce, I want to emphasize two things: you don't stay married in an unhealthy relationship for the sake of the kids or for the sake of money or to use the marriage to hold someone hostage.

That's not going to work. And on the other hand, I do believe that people in a marriage should do everything that they can, including counseling, to work it out, to catch it before it gets really bad. And if you're looking at another person, and having thoughts about that other person, well, hello! That means something is wrong in your marriage. You don't go looking for something unless it's already missing.

I do not believe in affairs. I will not go near a married man. There is a personal responsibility not to go behind your mate's back and have an affair. It's very damaging.

My parents' divorce is a situation I want to address up front. People judged my father, they judged Cindy, and they gave him a bad rap. It was just simply Dad was burnt out on the marriage and didn't know any other way, other than to leave the marriage. That was his judgment.

Ridicule followed. My brother's personal judgment, in a movie he made called *The Father I Knew*, was that it was a sin. I'm a Christian, born-again too, but I don't believe in judging others, and so I don't want to judge my brother. I understand where he was coming from. As a teenager, a young teenager, fourteen or fifteen years old, it was a very painful separation. And my brother's movie was from his personal perspective.

But I'm coming from a mature perspective that shows me that the way Dad handled it was not good. However, we cannot judge him to be a bad person and

Cindy to be this blond bimbo, which was what she was called, because that isn't fair. It's coming from a judgment that was built on people's personal opinions.

They didn't know that my mother had changed significantly, getting caught up into the Beverly Hills aristocratic lifestyle that really was against everything my father was. And, she changed into a better person afterward. It's not fair to judge somebody when you haven't walked in their shoes and felt their pain and experiences. It applies in all areas of life.

It may be that Dad should have left my mother, but not that way. But he didn't see it like that until later. Emotionally, he was in pain and blinded, and running in fear. You know, we're always either in love or in fear. Dr. Jerry Jampolsky just says it as clearly as that.

And Dad was in so much fear! His publicity, his fans, the kids. He was so confused. I don't think he had the opportunity to really think things out clearly. He even said it. "I'm so messed up. I don't know what I'm doing." And that was his humanness. He was gone overnight.

We act in bizarre ways sometimes. We do strange things. We're human. We run from fear, and fear chases us. We think by changing a family, or changing a home, that everything's going to be different, only to find out that fear's right there because we didn't change the core belief.

He had succeeded, but he was afraid he was missing whatever was the core. And he kept running. What I'm focusing on here is that I want people to stop, look, and choose before they run like my dad ran, because it did leave a lot of hurt feelings and unfinished business. And I do believe with all my heart the kids suffer the most. Instead of running, I think he could have talked to my mom and worked it out. He could have said, "You're an aristocrat and you're acting very spoiled and I'm to blame because I've spoiled you." And maybe they could have gone to counseling and they could have changed their lifestyle. Or maybe they would have discovered that they were at a point where they didn't get along. But at least he would have handled it with respect.

So they had a horrible, very ugly, public divorce. It was awful, what they went through. The attorneys really made my parents turn against each other.

Dad couldn't handle confrontations. I don't think too many of us who come from abusive backgrounds are good at handling confrontations. Because you're so used to being beaten, you go back to that little child who was beaten and screamed at, and you shut down. I'm always working on it myself. So really that would have been a very big thing for him to do.

When he had a choice about leaving his marriage, the mistake he made was not in leaving, but in the way that he left. He found no way to do it that involved truth between people. He ran. And he hurt my brothers and sisters and myself. He hurt my mother. He hurt so many people. If he could have found a way to follow his own principle of truth between people, it would not have left the scars it did. He still would have been gone, but it would have been a clean break. It probably would have left a positive feeling with my mother rather than devastation.

And he recognized that. When he was dying, I snuck into the house and my dad and I had some incredible conversations. He said, "I'm so sorry that I brought the baggage into the relationships and I know that how I left your mother was wrong. And I have suffered for it."

18

You have a choice of how you're going to react to a situation. But people aren't aware of that. Dad wasn't aware of that. If he had been, there could have been a whole different situation. And that's why I want people not to waste time, not to have to experience cancer to realize that we have choices and we can live a deliberate life. Even if they've had bad childhoods their lives are not set in such a way that they are ruined.

My mother's is a classic story about that. My mother had been this princess, whom Dad called an aristocrat. She said there was nothing to prepare her for this loss. It was like being at the top of the ladder, and then falling so hard to the bottom, with nothing between the top and the bottom. She hit bottom so hard that she had the choices to commit suicide, to become a drug addict, to become an alcoholic, to abandon us, or to take another route. And she took another route, and I'm very proud of my mother.

She became a born-again Christian, and it was that which gave her a strong sense of who she was. She and Jackie Joseph created a support group called LADIES: Life After Divorce Is Eventually Sane.

They went around to these other women while their own lives were being publicly displayed in the tabloids, while people were criticizing her. You know: "how much money she was given," and "what a rich bitch," and "how dare she, she doesn't know what it was really like to struggle." But she had lost the man of her life, the love of her life, the whole existence that she was dedicated to building. I mean she had even forgotten about us so that she could build Dad. Her whole focus was on Dad, and he was gone. And there she was, left empty, destroyed, humiliated. And she took that horrible pain and transformed it into positive opportunity to help other women.

She turned the situation around, because you can choose how you're going to react to a situation. And that's the key.

## 19

Moments before he was going to die, my father said, "Well guys, this is it. I'm not going to be here tomorrow. Is there anything you want to know? Now is the time to ask me."

And I spoke up from the group and said, "Dad, what is it that you want us to do that you haven't told us?"

He said, "Love one another."

## 20

After Dad died, we learned that his will had been changed to give the vast bulk of the estate to Cindy and her children, leaving the rest of us with small settlements. This puzzled and hurt us. Did it mean that Dad had ceased to love us? And of course, the resulting controversy made huge, uncomfortable publicity for all of us.

I decided to learn what I could about the circumstances of the change in the will. I interviewed many people about Dad's last days. What I discovered I chose to keep private, respecting Dad's memory and love for us, hoping that Cindy and I could work out our differences as Dad would have wanted. What I learned removed the hurtful suspicions that Dad had ceased to love us.

But my anger didn't go away. My bitterness didn't go away. I felt like Cindy had most of the money that Dad had accumulated over all those years, and neither Mom, who had helped him create it, nor his other children were to get any of it. I had to struggle daily to deal with my feelings, fighting hard not to be consumed with hatred and a desire for revenge. Cindy and I did not speak to each other for about three years.

I went through much emotional and physical anguish, to the point that I had big welts and fevers and clumps of my hair were falling out. My mother said, "Cheryl, it's not affecting her, it's affecting you." I prayed, and heard my father very clearly saying to me, "I will take care of her. Do not take revenge. I will take care of it."

## 21

And here's where God works in mysterious ways. Cindy was a big fan of Tony Robbins, and I had known him for the past seven years. His seminars had enabled me to get on stage and to deliver my own seminars.

She and I were publicly known to be in such a huge fight with each other, but our children had gone to Viewpoint school together, as my father had wished. So we would bump into each other and start talking. My father connected us because one thing that we had in common was the love for Michael Landon.

So I said, "You know, I'd like to work this out with you. And it takes two to work out a solution," and she responded. In our conversations, she had mentioned Tony Robbins and how much she liked him. And Tony Robbins had been instrumental in assisting me through my stage work, seven years ago, and he had become a very special mentor and friend to me.

Well, we wound up going to his three-day firewalk, scheduled over Memorial Day weekend, 1997.

On that particular event, you had to walk across twenty feet of literally burning coals. The theory behind it is that you are to face your worst fear, and what greater fear than burning your feet, let alone your body. To walk over hot coals, you are forced to elevate yourself to a higher consciousness. It demonstrates that the whole physiology is based on the state of our being. If we are in an elevated consciousness, a higher state of consciousness, we can walk over hot coals and not burn ourselves. And if we can walk over hot coals, then we can apply that to every single area in our lives that is a challenge. So it's facing our fear, conquering it, and knowing that we have the ability to do something that we're scared to death of.

Well, there we were at this firewalk. Tony had the firemen there and it was very dramatic. There were twenty lines of these coal beds lined up because he has a lot of people at these seminars. He gets everybody in this real high frenzy, and I can see why, all over the world, where they practice this firewalk, they have people dancing to drums so they can really get into an altered state.

Cindy had gone over the hot coals. But it didn't work for me. It just didn't work. I was not into that. I was not into pounding my chest and screaming as loud as I could. In fact, I resisted it. But what got to me was when he brought out the live drums and people started the African drumming. I started dancing. Now mind you, this is someone who was told she could never dance again.

I danced the most fantastic African dancing, just resonating to this drum, and I got into an altered state. And it was at this point that I heard Tony booming over the microphone, "Is there anybody who hasn't walked over the coals yet?"

## 22

I was very ready. The coals represented all the anger that I had inside, the revenge and the hatred because of what had happened to us with my father's estate, the lies, the betrayal, the hurt. The revenge and the hatred and the resentment of the injustice of everything was keeping me from moving forward with my life. So I used it symbolically.

Well, I did go over the hot coals. The next day I sat with Cindy, and we were together throughout the entire three days. And in this one exercise that got us in touch with the inner person, I experienced my father coming into me so strongly and it hit Cindy at the same time. I felt Dad's presence unlike I have ever felt it. Big, big, immense presence of Dad, bringing Cindy and me together. And all of a sudden, I just started sobbing.

They were tears of forgiveness. It was this release, this huge breakthrough. And I know Dad was there, and I know Dad was sharing the love that brought Cindy and me together. And it was the one common denominator that truly brought us together. Not only brought us together, but broke down that big barrier of being hurt and betrayed and wanting revenge and every negative conflict that I was facing. It all melted down. We looked at each other, and we were both crying in each other's arms, genuinely saying, "I love you. I forgive you. Please forgive me."

And that, to me, is the power of love. When you are feeling so challenged by an issue, it always involves people. When it's within our families it hurts even more, because that's our source of security. When you come across that in your family, it is just such a feeling of betrayal and hurt.

Some people choose to hold grudges. But my dad always wanted us to work out our differences. He always wanted people who had issues to forgive and to move on. He was very big on that. He was constantly telling us that it's very important to open your arms up, not to hold grudges, to work it out.

And to feel this release, this breakthrough, melt into pure joy and forgiveness was the most powerful moment that I had experienced with Cindy Landon. I believe it was equally strong for her, because we both felt Dad at the same moment.

I can't explain it. It was a feeling of this tremendous warmth and love that was unconditional. It was the purest feeling of love, and it brought tears, sobbing tears. You couldn't fake it. You couldn't fake it. We had both looked at each other at the same moment and held each other closely, sobbing, and just saying, "I love you so much." And there lies the turning point; the crossroads had been reached. But the turning point had been directed through our willingness to work out our differences. I tell people, you don't have to walk over twenty feet of hot, burning coals. You can simply extend a hand, pick up the phone, and say, "Let's talk."

## 23

Now, this didn't solve any of the actual issues between us. But what happened was that Cindy began sponsoring a portion of my work, which has been valuable because it was symbolic of reaching her hand out to me and saying, "I believe in what you're doing and I want to be a part of supporting what you are doing."

I had to learn that, whatever went down, went down; and I had to move on. I probably will never see my rightful inheritance, but what I see is that there is a clean slate. I see that the doors that have opened in my work are truly the work of God. I feel my dad's guiding hands in it. People have come, opportunities have come, that demonstrate to me the power of love in action—because I chose to take the high road. If I had taken the low road, and carried on with the resentment, the anger, the revenge, I would be hurting myself. It truly is an action that comes back and strikes you ten times as hard.

I am making a distinction between my opinions, which may be the same, and my feelings, which changed. I choose to see the goodness in Cindy, and she chooses to see the goodness in me. So, when I talk to people on the road about things like this, they too may have issues that cannot be resolved physically, but they can change their feelings. It is always in their power. And that's the focus. The focus and the shift of perception is the miracle.

Again I come back to Cindy's children—who happen to be my brother and sister—and my son. They represent the future generation, and I don't want them to hate. I don't want them to feel this pain. I want to believe that there is a higher power and action and so, whoever perpetrates whatever negative action will have that returned to them. That is not my business anymore. That was a very big learning curve for me.

It was a huge crisis and it affected all of us and it affects our children. I'm still fighting fear on a daily basis and I fight not getting sucked into hatred and wanting revenge, because I can always find a lot of excuses. How come my future isn't secure? How come my son's future isn't secure with that vast estate? We were given a six-figure amount that was so unfair, but we are not here to judge it. I am not here to judge it but to use it to my advantage.

## 24

My own work started as a promise that I made to my dad on his deathbed. He told me, "Cheryl, I cannot die. Society is self-destructing. Our youth, our future generation doesn't stand a chance, and I'm the one who will make a difference."

That was his serious call to us. I knew that this was so important to Dad.

When we found out that he had three weeks to live, I started to write him letters every day that I wasn't with him. He called me at home and said, "Now you're coming to see me, aren't you?" I loved those phone calls. And I would go visit him on the weekend. And I remember lying on the bed and I would read all the cards to him that I had written. This one particular time, I wrote him that I promised to honor and protect his name and to continue

his legacy—his work to secure a healthy future generation—and to dedicate it in his memory.

Why is it that so much of my significance still ties
into my father? I feel his loss deeply. And I still feel very
vulnerable. I did not understand why I felt so insecure
until I realized how much my significance was tied into
my father. I would have done anything for him, which is
both good and bad.

It's good because the man gave me a life that no one
on this earth would ever give me, and he asked so little. He
was the easiest man to please. So I would do anything for
him, as I'm doing these past years, keeping my promise to
him. But I realized how attached I am to him for security
and significance. So much of me is wrapped up in memories of him. There isn't a day that I don't miss him.
Carrying on this work has been the hardest, most
challenging effort I've ever made. It is because of his love
and his wish that I'm doing all I'm doing. But I'm owning
it too. I get a sense that I am supported by him still, but
now it really is support. Now I'm the one on stage.

The first obstacle to starting the tour was having lies
perpetuated about me, that I was the "unofficial daughter," exploiting my father to make money. It was printed in
*TV Guide.* It affected my reputation. It made it difficult to
get on talk shows. Instead, I got the tabloids calling me,
wanting to pay me to talk. It was a big-time temptation. I
needed money to keep this work going. I could have taken

the easy way out. I would have had a tremendous amount of material security, but it goes against what I'm doing on a spiritual level. I wouldn't have been able to be the person I wanted to be. I would have sold out on myself. I would have become one of the others. Likewise, if I had given in to having a relationship with a man who was not in agreement with my work, I would have sold out to marry a very wealthy man and give up the work.

And then came my first book, *I Promised My Dad*—and the seminars, because I love to teach. Nothing had been handed to me. I worked very, very hard and if I had known how hard this was going to be, I wouldn't have been able to take it on. It would have scared me. On the other hand, it's such a strong passion and drive that I just knew I had to do it.

Next came radio, and then television, and back to touring and doing live shows. I suppose people think, "Oh, she's riding on her dad's coattails." Well, I'm riding on my dad's coattails in the way that, say, Coretta Scott King is with Martin Luther King's. It's not kicking back and saying, "Okay, I'm a princess and I'm Michael Landon's daughter and you're going to hire me." That is not how it works. I'm competing with over 100,000 people in live seminars, in America alone. It's very competitive.

So my chances of getting a show are very low unless I have a bestseller. I know I have that ability. My confidence is very strong. It's been nine years, and I've been very close at times to giving up and just taking a job that really is not within my love and passion, a regular nine-to-five job. Then an opportunity comes, and it's like I'm meant to be on this road. It has not been easy. If I'd had my inheritance, then I wouldn't have had all this worry and struggle and challenge to make it work. But I might not have done it at all. So there is a higher intelligence working.

## 25

Many people have come up to me asked, "How do you know that your father is in the hereafter?" They are usually people who have experienced the loss of a loved one. And I tell them that, if we look for the signs, truly, life is a roadmap and it's just full of heavenly divine signs. But we walk around with blinders on. We're only focused on seeing certain things and we're missing all the beauty that surrounds us. I specifically asked my father to show me demonstrations. And I believe anybody can have a demonstration.

One time, I was in my bathroom and I had asked and prayed for a demonstration. Now mind you, prayer is a method of communicating with God, of communicating with your loved one. So there isn't a specific ritual that you have to follow. That is a very personal time and experience.

I needed these signs. You see, I felt like I had been thrown into the lion's den with a peashooter after my dad had made his passing. There were devastating embezzlement issues. It was devastating to have everything stolen or somehow taken away through whatever legal measures. And to be without my father has been a very frightening position.

This was in 1993. I had been working on stage, delivering live seminars, but my ignorance, my naïveté, was awful in business. I learned that my business manager had gone through $250,000 for himself. And overnight, I found out that I was broke. I had been touring and working, and all the money I had made was gone.

I was ready to call it quits and jump over a cliff. I just couldn't believe that this had happened to me. Besides losing my dad, besides losing the inheritance, besides thinking that now I had gotten clear about Dad and his love for us, now this. I has been working my tush off touring and traveling—and they're ungodly hours. The reward is phenomenal because I love people. I love giving the message. I love the interaction. But to have four hours of sleep for many nights in a row, to be on the road all the time, to always be at your peak best, takes a lot of determination. It's taxing on the body. It's taxing on the mind. And I come home and I need to be a full parent.

And then everything I had worked so hard to regain was gone overnight.

So I'm in my bathroom praying and before my eyes I see this black blob appear on a dry white facecloth hanging on my shower. I was standing there, and right before my eyes, there's this black blob. It started manifesting into the shape of a bird, ready to take flight. My father had told Cindy and me, separately, that he would come in the form of a bird. And I saw this blob forming this beautiful picture. I didn't paint it. I didn't do anything. This occurred. I have it framed. And it was proof, a demonstration.

## 26

I took it as a sign, and went back and got involved. In fact, that's when Women's Federation for World Peace came into my life.

I had been touring for the book *I Promised My Dad*, and all the money from that was gone overnight. Then I got a phone call from a contact from the *Washington Times*. She said, "Are you interested in world peace?"

I said, "Totally."

She said, "I think I've got a job for you." And then I began the most incredible work with Women's Federation for World Peace. I have toured for six years and been involved in one of the most promising and meaningful causes, with women from all around the world coming together to stand up for world peace—to give our future children a healthy generation.

It's about reconciliation and forgiveness. There are women from Japan, with whom I did a six-city tour there. I have donated my time but I also had the opportunity to speak and be formally paid as a professional speaker. I have to tell you, I am so on fire from the motivation and the enthusiasm of international women, mothers, coming together for peace for our children. That is an emotional charge.

We've been doing it with what we call the Bridge of Peace Walk. There literally is a bridge and we took it all around the United States to coliseums. The intention is to face what is symbolic of your enemy. At the time, it was an anniversary of the bombing of Pearl Harbor.

And the Japanese and the Americans—they didn't speak English and we didn't speak Japanese—would stand on the bridge and we would cross it, so full of divine spirit that tears would come down our eyes as we bowed to one another. We bowed to one another as symbol of forgiveness and reconciliation. We would hold hands, and we would bond as sisters. And I've done this in high schools and colleges where we've gotten into some of the worst gang rivalries. We put the gangs on either side of the bridge, beginning with the mothers first, bowing to each other. See, the power of mothers is fantastic. The mothers go first, then the children go, the teenagers go, the college students go.

The Hispanic community and the Black community and the White community—all of us were there, and we bowed to one another. I love it because we are setting an example—a positive example for people to come together under the simplicity of honoring one another.

The speakers go first, so you're put into a state of witnessing a change, to know that you are a part of history, part of a movement that is focused on peace, reconciliation through the power of love and forgiveness. And you cannot hate when you have vowed to reconcile, and have made a commitment to forgive and to create friendships for our future generation.

First, we would have speakers like Coretta Scott King, who is one of my favorites. I love this woman because she's the authentic person. She just emanates an energy that fills the whole room. She is so spiritually filled that you can only feel and experience the positive energy. And her words are so powerful. It's like an extension, the support of Martin Luther King Jr., whom I love.

Former President Bush and Barbara Bush brought this over to the United States. It was their idea, with Reverend Sun Myung Moon and his wife, Dr. Hak Ja Han Moon, who own the *Washington Times*. Reverend Moon has gotten a really bad rap, but he's a great, great person. So is Dr. Moon, his wife. These are good people. People used to call their followers "Moonies." I'm not a Moonie, but I'm very proud that I was a member of Women's Federation for

World Peace. I have tremendous respect for these people because they're into positive journalism, family, and spreading the word of God. We get into judgment here, but I look at their actions, and their actions were creating peace.

Barbara Bush, our former first lady, reminds me of the mother of America. What you see is what you get. She is very grounded in solid roots. I have respect for her. We can be grounded in solid, positive roots of love or we can be grounded in solid roots of fear.

Barbara Bush has such positive roots that she stood up to people making fun of her for wearing the clothes that she wore, or being a big, grand woman. I loved her because she opened up her jacket and she said, "You know, I get teased about the clothes that I wear, but what you see is what you get."

She is authentic.

And I want all of us to feel authentic and proud of who we are and where we're at. That's being in the moment.

## 27

Janice Cooper Wilson is the current wife to my ex-husband and the stepmother to my son, James Michael. Her daughters, Schyler and Shambri, are my goddaughters.

This is about finding God in each other. Where we could have hated each other and torn each other down and kept these barriers which would have devastated our children, we instead took the high road and found tremendous, grander meaning—greater purpose together. And it is such a blessing because we found God in each other. Besides being very good friends, I consider her my sister and it's just been a bigger happy family. I believe any broken family can duplicate this by coming from the heart to find God and going beyond the ego.

Because we share a strong devotion to God and a mission for the youth, we have formed a partnership. Here is where Janice and I are going with our work: Our vision is to expand to the point where we can launch positive television programs, positive radio programs, positive products under US (United Spiritually) Entertainment. It was Janice who came up with the name, "United Spiritually."

We're in production with a television series and a movie based on my book, *I Promised My Dad.* The television series, *Pennies from Heaven,* is under the umbrella of US Entertainment.

Our mission statement is to raise one healthy generation and create an alignment to heal our world. So this is the power of us joining together. Now we have joined in vision and joined in partnering. We're bringing in modern-day music, hip-hop. Not corny, not vulgar. We're going to be doing a fifty-state high school tour called "Excel to Improve." It's just going into the schools for one period in a school day, and we'll be in a different school more or less every day for six months. We're doing this because we want to launch the positive messages. We're talking to the youth about making positive choices. I'm the emcee and I give a speech. Then Janice's girls, my goddaughters, will be entertaining and singing and dancing under the name of "Brésha," along with an entourage of today's hottest youthful celebrities.

Part of the message of my present tour stems from what I observed in my father. He passed solid character basics on to me. He had such a strong will and determination, such a great work ethic. He was honest. He built what I call universal values upon compassion:

- That love is truly the most powerful force in our universe.
- That how we view ourselves does affect who we become.
- That there should be truth between people and within ourselves.
- That we are in God's image and that there is God in all of us.
- That we should be good to people, respecting one another.
- That we are here to bring out the best in one another.

These are universal, basic values. Anybody can follow them. You don't have to follow a certain religion or belief. They are self-evident once they are stated. You know they're true. It's just a matter of keeping it simple.

My father always said that, if we could just speak in simple terms, people could understand us. Some people use huge words to try to show off their intelligence. But the person who can touch another person's heart with simple truth, who states truth as it is, is much more intelligent.

And that's exactly what my dad did with his television shows. They were simple shows that everybody gets, because he used universal values. And that's why, nine years later, they're going stronger than ever. No one can touch what he did. We have not seen another Michael Landon. That's why I say he was a prophet.

## 28

Our thinking causes things to happen. We need to wake up and realize the power of our thinking, the power of our focus. We have been told, "It is done unto you as you believe," and this is true. If you are thinking about the difficulty, you are going to focus on the difficulty. You are going to *attract* the difficulty.

I am a person who has experienced a tremendous amount of pain, a tremendous number of setbacks, and it's a challenge not to get sucked into the darkness of wanting revenge. But the love of my mission, and my son, and who I am has brought me to this point—where I am experiencing a greater life and a grander purpose.

My intention is to get people back to the simplicity of who we are. Life is not about just suffering or struggling. The belief system is like a computer. You get answers according to your beliefs. You put in the ideas, you access them with the right questions, and you get the right answers. We need to start asking better-quality questions, focusing on better-quality thoughts.

If we realize the power that is within our minds, we focus on magnificence instead of destruction. Using our mind in a new way creates an evolution: that mind is thought; and how we access this thought creates our growth.

God is good and good is God. If I start to see the God in everyone, then I will bring out the good in my life. We must be patient, but very determined. I want so much to raise one healthy generation, and I'm challenging all of us to change the way we are acting. Start becoming a deliberate person who makes powerful, positive choices to seek the God in everyone. That is the only way that I have had my healings: the tremendous healing with Cindy, the tremendous healings in my family and with my ex-husband.

Don't waste time hating one another. It doesn't work. It will only take you down.

Suggestion is very powerful. That is what Michael Landon wanted us to get in touch with. The power of how we love one another is truly bringing out the best in one another. The seven keys that follow are brought to you with genuine authenticity, and tremendous love and devotion—from the greatest legacy of love, which I claim as my rightful inheritance. And that is the love of Michael Landon—which he gave to me, which I am now passing on to you.

Dear reader, love is everybody's inheritance. We are all chosen ones. We are all miracles. You and I are here to love one another. Love is what we inherit, and love is what we are to pass on to our children. That is the legacy.

# Part Two:
# The Seven Keys

# About the Seven Keys

The seven keys came out of nine years of hardship and loss and not giving up.

I want people to be happy right now where they're at in their lives, because I have noticed in others—and within myself—a way of thinking that says things would be fine "if only" I had more money, or "if only" I had a better relationship, or "if only" I had a better job. There's a curse in that way of thinking: It keeps us out of the here and now.

*This* is the most precious time, the best opportunity that we have. To be present—to be *in* the present—is to be alive with grace and joy. People need to know that what you have in your life right now is perfect. This doesn't mean you don't want to change anything, it means putting things into perspective. It is normal and natural to want to have a better life, a better job, a better income, a better relationship, a better future for your children. But don't live in depression rather than experiencing and rejoicing in life. Don't let "wants" make you blind to the here and now.

There is more power, more happiness in enjoying this day. I am often tempted to say, "Oh, if only I had that perfect relationship, if only I had that mansion that I grew up in, if only I had my dad." But that would rob me of what I have right now, including a beautiful boy who is turning into a wonderful young man—who, in a couple of years, isn't going to be at home. The words "if only, if only" keep us out of who we are right here and right now.

The first time I ever experienced being right here and right now was at CEDU, in a twenty-four-hour pro-feed session on "The Truth Will Set You Free." All my life I had been comparing myself to my mother's expectations. She had a better figure, and she was always saying if only you had better legs, if only you had a bigger top, etc. "If only, if only," and so I really didn't feel good enough as I was. In the middle of that pro-feed, I got rid of that idea that I had to be someone other than myself.

I ask myself how it was that I wound up with one parent who continually said "if only," and another parent who said "you're great right as you are." I really don't know the answer, because life is a mystery and God works in mysterious ways. But maybe we attract these issues into our lives so that we can grow into better people. If I had allowed "if only" to control me, I would not be confident doing what I'm doing now; but if I had never had the *if onlys*, I wouldn't know what it was like to have had *if onlys*, and I couldn't relate to the everyday person struggling.

I was fortunate to have somebody to mirror that way of being, so that I learned that it isn't such a productive way of being. But it took me a long time to get beyond that thinking, and I think a lot of people are caught up in it. I hear people saying, "I don't get along with my brother," or "I don't get along with my mother," or "They don't think I'm good enough." In situations like that, it's more productive to focus on what we have in common with that person—whom we do love—than to focus on the opposite. Focus on love, and when others say hurtful things, rise above it. Take the high road. Say, "Okay, that's their opinion, but I don't think of myself like that, so it's not going to hurt me like it used to." Let it roll over you like water off a duck's back. Just let it roll right over you. Don't get caught up in it.

I believe we all have guardian angels in our lives. In all our lives, there is a mentor somewhere. It may be your teacher, your next-door neighbor, the janitor, anybody. Even suppose you grew up in a situation like Michael Landon grew up in, with nobody in the family giving any kind of love. There is a mentor. Go to the higher self and trust in God. Live your life knowing that we are protected, that we all have these guardian angels in our lives. How do you know that a guardian angel isn't already in your life? If you're closed off in the blinding darkness of pain and fear, you cannot see the guardian angel right there next to you. When you're open to it, it comes to you. Trust in God.

The bottom line is "who I am" versus "who am I?" "Who I am" is very grounded. You don't question who you are because you know that you are a part of God. And if you don't understand who "God" is, think merely of the higher power that created us and the world. Look up and see the stars. Those stars are in perfect order. There is no way that you can look up at the stars and say there is no God. When you go outside, instead of going to the mailbox, and saying, "Oh, I'm going to get bills and I just hate bills," look around you. You can see colors. Or if you can't see colors, you can at least smell and feel the wind. This is the natural order. When you know the higher power exists, there's no question that there is a higher power in us that created us. To those who say "prove God exists," I offer the mere fact that we're breathing, the mere fact that we do see colors, that we can hear, that we can feel the wind. You don't see the wind, but it's there.

Some people say, "There's a higher power that created the world, but that higher power can't possibly be interested in me. I'm just a little individual." That is "who am I?" speaking. "Who I am" knows that "who I am" is grounded in this power. There's just no way that God would create all of these things—flowers, trees, rainbows, water, cats, dogs, birds—and not have a purpose for man.

All this is easy once you have had the direct experience of it. Until then—well, sometimes we've got to start by taking a step in faith until we experience it ourselves.

Sometimes you've got to start at that point, as I did. The first time I began to experience God was when my dad saved me from further physical abuse in my biological father's family. To experience love was to experience God. I didn't make the mental connection then; I just knew, inside. It was that leap of faith.

Michael Landon had every reason to be angry at the world, to be bitter. Yet he taught us about the power of love, because he knew that there was a greater meaning in life. We hear about kids who have been abused (I believe that's part of their past karma that they're working through, and that they have an opportunity to begin anew). Whatever we came into this life with are things that are unfinished business—that we have the opportunity to finish. It's how we finish them that gives us the control over our lives right here and right now. We're here to choose. Those kids need to know that.

In my talks to school kids, I get their attention by saying "you're all going to die." Then, to try to teach them that they are part of God and can trust Him, I share my own personal experience, which is all that I *can* share with them. I use it so that they can learn from it. And if I'm willing to be honest about myself, then they know it's true, because people know the truth when they hear it. I share with them that I was not pro-God all my life, that I hated God; I thought there was no God who loved me. And they relate to that.

I tell them that their instincts are built into higher intuition, that learning to trust ourselves is one step toward getting to know God, as you are a part of God. Life is like an ocean, in that you have times of storms and times of quietness. Life stirs up the "cosmos chips" and lets them fall where they fall. (It's a saying from CEDU: Let the cosmos chips fall where they fall.) In the time of the storm you must be quiet, and doing that is really hard unless someone teaches you how. How better to teach them than through stories? So I share my experiences. I tell them to wake up and realize that we have control of our own destiny through the power of our choices.

Everything has a starting point. If, when I was a teenager, I had had this wisdom, I'm sure my life would have been completely different. But that is a part of growing up. That's why we need to be taught. And that's why we're coming out with these seven keys, so that we can teach people in a very simple manner, how to get from A to Z.

When my dad was growing up as Eugene Orowitz, in Collingswood, New Jersey, what were thought of as Christian values sometimes led to anti-Semitism. And that was wrong. Trying to enforce any one set of values is wrong. But then we went to the extreme and took God out of the schools completely, even taking discussion of God completely out. We need to bring spirituality back to the schools, but we have to bring it back in a sophisticated way, an open-minded way, not trying to put people into a certain religion, but preaching a spirituality that is non-denominational.

I love the spirituality behind the seven keys because it's open to all generations, cultures, races, nationalities. It's inclusive of all—every single person. It's not saying, "If you don't believe in Jesus Christ then you're going to Hell; and if you're a Hindu, you shouldn't be here." That's where we went wrong. I believe that religion can have a tendency to use fear to control people. Parts of religion are very fear-oriented. But I don't believe that that's of God. What is of God is of love, and it's all-inclusive.

Let everybody be who they are. Let them follow whatever religion they choose to, as long as it's not violating and hurting another person. With all my heart, I believe that there is a higher intelligence within us, but we have been blinded to using it. The higher intelligence knows right from wrong, knows when you're hurting someone, knows when you're cheating, knows when you're lying. And, likewise, you know it yourself. Just trusting that simple thought makes us able to differentiate between making a lower conscious choice—a poor choice—or a higher conscious choice. Sometimes people find themselves unable to see things clearly. That's why I think stories are very powerful. If I can use stories as my father used stories, there's no confusion.

"Trust in God" is the number one key that we start with. In my own situation, I could have related to the hurt and the pain or I could have related to the God conscious-ness and goodness. If I keep focusing on the goodness and the God consciousness, without being a wimp—because it takes a lot of courage to come from God consciousness rather than being sucked into hatred—I know that my light is truth, and that resonates to the other person. Pure truth. Not a fake truth.

When you're dealing with other people, whatever the situation, you can have confidence that your life is not under their control, but under your control. And that's important. I see so many people who depend on money to make them feel powerful. But that's putting things in the wrong order. It should be God and then money, because if I focus on God as the creative source of money, then I'm going to look to you with integrity and love. I'm going to know that I am in a power far greater than any power in this universe. Which, again, takes you out of fear. And fear is crippling.

In my nine years of being on tour, I have seen that a lot of people do not realize the power of their minds. In my seminars, I go through my experience and I ask the participants, "What three beliefs do you hold about your-self that keep you locked into fear? What would you like to change right now? List three situations that are tied into three fears that you react from."

After they write them down, I say, "Okay. This is what controls your life."

It's a new idea to them.

And then I say, "You have the ability to change that into freedom. You have the power of choice. You can gain control of that fear. This is how you do it. . . ." The Second Key is to "Choose Love over Fear."

We have to become aware of our fear. If I am scared to address an issue with somebody who is hurting me, then something is going on within me that's keeping me feeling inferior. So, I need to build up my confidence first, and then confront. But I need to stand by what my feelings are. I could say, "You really hurt me when you talk like that," or I could say "I'm never going to see you again. I can't stand you." There is a big choice. Now, why would I feel like saying, "I never want to see you again"? Because something in me is keeping me inferior, rather than building me as a positive person. And God knows how many years you miss because of all those days of built-up resentment eating you up. When you're coming from a secure place, you can eliminate it within *minutes* rather than days, months, and years.

If you have been taught how to come from a secure place, you don't have to act out of fear. If not, you may not have any alternative but fear, and then you project it on everybody else. "You made me do this." That's what happened with my dad when he left my mother. However, I learned from that. And that's what this book is about. We are here to teach one another. The purpose of this book is to bring out these issues so that people start taking total, deliberate responsibility—living life deliberately.

I want to say this in even simpler terms. The fears that we resist are exactly what persists in our lives. My biological father was jealous, out of fear that Michael Landon and I were going to be close and that I wouldn't love him as much as I loved Michael Landon. So that is exactly what happened. And it happened as a result of his actions, which were based in the fear of that happening.

Our "issues" are all set in fear in one way or another. You're either in love or you're in fear. No fears, no issues. You're either in love or you're in fear. These keys apply to all of us in this whole wide world: the rich, the poor, the meek, the strong—every single class, color, race, nation—all of us.

All of our woes, all of our tragedies, are brought into our lives because we are *attracting* them into our lives. Even, God forbid, the death of your child, which is one of the worst things I can imagine happening. Everyone has made choices. So, instead of looking at the negative side, we must be deliberate in choosing the spiritual side. The Third Key is: "Believe that Daily Miracles Do Occur."

We are all miracles, we are all chosen ones. Once we realize that, it takes us on to a higher consciousness. And in this state, we reflect positive thoughts. In turn, we vibrate at a higher level. Vibrations, like sound waves, affect other people. Have you ever walked into a room with a low energy level, and seen one person, up in a higher vibration, affect other people? That happened with Michael Landon all the time. Energy is very powerful. We can *choose* to have high energy or low energy. Even though I'm in chronic pain all the time, I can get into a higher consciousness, and vibrate at a higher energy level all the time. Anybody can do this.

What we focus on is what we get. If we're focusing on the idea that we are losers, worthless—all the negative, fearful things—then that is exactly what we are going to attract into our life. And if we focus on the fact that we are miracles, that we are all chosen ones, we're going to attract a whole different consciousness—in even the worst of situations. This has happened in my life. I have had tremendous healings with Cindy and with my mother. For years, I hated my biological father, but we are friends now. I shifted my consciousness and they responded.

If I can do it, anybody can do it. If Michael Landon can do it, anybody can do it. Having once been in a psychiatric hospital, I later went back to teach. I worked with kids who, like me, had tried to commit suicide. I planted seeds.

I would have them use their imagination. I'd say, "Just close your eyes and sit and imagine that you're all that you want to be. How would your higher self look? How would your higher self feel? What would you be doing? How would your body posture be? Envision that. Be it." I had them start identifying with that person.

Then I'd ask them, "How do you feel when you are accepting yourself as a loser?" And when they had done that, I would ask, simply, "Which one would you prefer to attach yourself to?" So now they know they have a choice. I had to do this for myself. Michael Landon had to envision that for himself. What we think is what we attract and become.

Everybody has this potential to be the victor, rather than the victim. The doctors told me that I was never going to have a child, that I would wind up crippled in a wheelchair, that really I was going to just be a burden. If I had bought that, I would be dead, or lying in some bed, depressed and loaded up on drugs. And I see a lot of people who are victims of pain—pain in relationships, in careers, in business, with their children, with themselves—and physical pain, big time. They buy it.

I am in a lot of pain. However, I have learned to rechannel the pain. These keys have enabled me to be a powerful woman, creating and working and loving. I have the most beautiful young man that God could ever give me. I was able to conceive and have a child, even though medically, there was no way I was supposed to be able to. It wasn't luck. There's no such thing as luck. It's about the mind. We create our own luck.

We—people, each individual person who is of God—we make it happen. Nobody else makes it happen for us. Our thinking is everything. Life is consciousness.

Every single thought that goes into our head. Take action over your thoughts. Take action over your fears because you are in control. The Fourth Key is: "Take Action Now."

Whatever the challenge is, instead of letting it control you, ride the challenge and discover what opportunity it is bringing you. Every day is a new beginning, a new opportunity to stop and renew. Take action to stop, look, choose, and renew. Renew yourself to the higher truth. To thine own Self be true—"Self" with a capital S.

Really, it's about the truth within yourself. It's just knowing that you have a polished diamond in the core of your being and all the junk that is surrounding it can be washed away. It's an ongoing action, every day. Every day, we have to take action to clean the junk off. Every day, we have to "Believe in Truth between People," the Fifth Key.

I don't have the security of a substantial amount of money in the bank, and I'm still not used to that. I was used to being taken care of in every way. Now, I have to work and I have to take care of my son and provide for his education. I have to be effective.

I still face health issues that can take me down any day. It's scary. If my health issues overtake me, who is going to take care of my son? So it's forcing me to trust in God rather than in a bank account. It's forcing me to trust myself to stay on that high road, to trust that I am capable of generating a good income and serving my mission and serving my promises to my dad.

Even though there have been times when I had no idea where I was going, or where security would come from, I have used these keys on a daily basis to stay on track and not get lured into hatred, or feeling like a victim. But I still have to deal with fears on a daily basis. I feel that I am more in alignment with the everyday people who live from paycheck to paycheck, who worry about their child's future, who are a part of the system. I no longer have my dad to go running to when I'm in trouble, and I don't have him to talk to. Before, when I had physical breakdowns, I knew that if anything happened to me, Dad would provide for my son, or if necessary even for me. I don't have that now. So I have to stay with these keys and be very grounded in what I am teaching to other people. It really forces me to practice what I preach, because there's no other way I can live, and there's no one I can depend on.

Yet I wonder, is there really a God, a Higher Force working for the higher good in my life? What does that mean when it's tough? Especially when others are stealing and lying for their personal gains. But I say to you, and I say to myself, that the way back home is to know "who I am," with a grander purpose. Tough times lead us to a greater purpose, greater meaning. They give us freedom, allowing us to do more with our lives than remaining stuck in a comfort zone.

In my work, I see that money is the number one issue. Money controls us until we learn to have faith that we have the ability to generate money, because money is God in action. I'm still going through it because I'm not at the point where I can kick back, relax, and feel the flow of money. But I'm learning that money is God in action.

What did it mean to me to go from having everything at my fingertips to losing everything? I could even lose custody of my son if I became unable to provide for him. I have had to build bridges to God, to know that God is in action and that the circulation of money is the circulation of God in action working in my life. To take my mind off worrying about money, and place it on the knowledge that God is working in my life, really shifts the perception of fear and worry into safety, security, and confidence.

A lot of people are in jobs they find to be without meaning. My dad could take all these odd jobs, like making ribbons and selling books and blankets and all that, and find a purpose, a significance. He wanted to make the best ribbons because he knew someone was going to be using them. The world is kept going by people who do humble jobs and do them as well as they can. If we can find purpose in whatever we do, knowing that God relies on us to take care of one another, this shifts the perception, and allows us to build bridges to one another to find what we have in common. What can I bring out in you which in turn brings it out in me? That's why hatred kills, and love builds. Our Sixth Key is: "Build Bridges."

With my son James Michael.

Dad taught me how to fish,
and took this picture
of my first catch.

The last picture
taken of Dad
before he died.
From left:
Jennifer, Leslie,
Shawna, Chris,
Cindy, and Dad.

Michael Jr., Dad, Mom, Leslie, and me at CEDU.

I met former First Lady Barbara Bush when we spoke to the Women's Federation for World Peace in Washington, D.C. Pictured from the left are Mrs. Sugiyuma, the president of the WFWP for Japan; me; Mrs. Bush; and Mrs. Nora Spurgin, President of the WFWP for the U.S.

At a meeting of the Women's Federation for World Peace in Los Angeles. From left: Suzanne Marx's aide Helene, Bernice (my cousin), Coretta Scott King, and me. Both Mrs. King and I were speakers.

The last funny-face family picture.

Shawna, me, and Leslie at our Beverly Hills home.

Dad making a funny face with James Michael and J.M.'s Uncle Sean (left), Dad's ninth child.

Mom and Dad in happy times.

The result of a positive divorce: James Michael with his two sisters Schyler and Shambri (my Goddaughters), and his stepmom Janice (my business partner).

My brother, Adam Pontrelli, and sister Beth Pontrelli, with a friend on my brother's graduation from college.

Leslie and me while I was at CEDU. Taken by Dad.

A manifestation: The unexplained blob that became a bird.

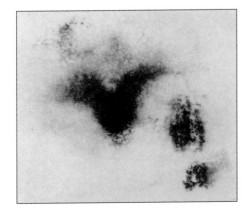

Funny faces at Leslie's wedding lunch: From left, Kaley, me, Leslie, sister-in-law Shar'ee, and Shawna.

Brother Chris and me with James Michael, the son the doctors said I would never be able to have.

Dad and his first grandchild, James Michael, with son-in-law Jim Wilson, my ex-husband and best friend.

Dad with Shawna and me. Love still goes on after divorce. We remained close to Dad.

My first book brought me letters from Dad's fans all over the world.

With one of my greatest role models. I appeared on Oprah's
show November 16, 1992, on my 39th birthday.

The fountain of the
Archangel Michael
in New York's
Central Park.

Holding the
long-stemmed rose.

During Dad's illness, the
Rodriguez sisters drove a
couple of hours every weekend
to put ribbons and encouraging
signs on the gate, which we
greatly appreciated.

To me, this demonstrates
the loyalty of Michael
Landon fans, who
inspire me to this day.
I love you all.

I'm choosing to build bridges to lift me up above a tough world of mistrust, rage, and greed, and to ask, "What beliefs am I embracing to attract these raging fires into my life?" Because that which we focus upon is that which we get, and it may be quite productive that you're bringing these fires into your life so that you can transcend them. That is part of growth. Nobody wants hard times, and yet the hard times are the best times. In fact my mom said that her best memories were those days when she and Dad were building his empire together.

My tours and my work build bridges to a different kind of people than I've ever been privileged to deal with. I have gained rewards that no money could buy. In fact money kept me away from it. When I'm in the seminars, people suddenly realize that their fears control them, and the big "Aha!" comes. They become like new people. I see it in their faces, and see them jumping up and down instead of standing with their shoulders hunched over, like they were when they walked into the seminar. To give them these keys, so that they realize that they're more empowered and they're more creative expressions of God—this is the greatest reward and meaning for me.

We need to strip ourselves down to the truth. The truth is that it's truly an illusion that we have created—an error in our thinking—to believe that "I am a victim," that "I am helpless and hopeless" and "I can't do anything" and "this person did this to me." All those fires raging within us are truly issues that we need to address within ourselves. We can straighten out and shift this thinking and get onto the high road.

We're challenged on a daily basis, moment to moment, and life gives us some very valid reasons to feel that it is full of tragedy and that we're victims. However, what we need to do is to judge only ourselves. How we judge ourselves is truly the most important judgment we can ever make. Instead of blaming and judging others, we need to learn how to embrace life, moving towards new awareness, new truth, and the opportunities that exist in each challenge. We need to know that God is always present, and that we are always choosing to turn on to God or to turn off from God. And that's the Seventh Key, "Don't Judge Each Other."

By judging the truths we hold about our own identities, we can go deep into our core beliefs about ourselves. This opens us up towards positive transformation, as opposed to judging someone else and saying that they're the problem. When Jesus said, "Turn the other cheek," he didn't mean turn the other cheek and have someone slap you on the other side. Jesus meant, "get a new attitude."

See, we're here to *experience* life. We're not here to run life, to be in our heads all the time. We're just here. We're spiritual beings in a human body, experiencing life. This is what people have to know. Future generations depend on us to make some major shifts in our perceptions.

My dad was a very simple person, with the ability to tap into his higher consciousness on a daily basis. And that's why I call him a prophet. He had the ability to take complex issues and break them into a simplicity that everyone could relate to. His stories touched people. And they still do.

Dad always fought his demons. And I relate to that because I still fight my demons, all stemming from my earliest childhood. That's why I have dedicated my life to this mission, because I understand the power of the first five or six years in forming our confidence. I implore all parents to raise their children with confidence, to say "I love you, I believe in you," to be a part of their lives, to make wise choices. It makes all the difference in the world. I tell my son all the time, "I believe in you, I love you, I'm here for you," because I went through such hell as a child, and so did Michael Landon. I'm forty-seven years old, and I still have to fight those demons: the fear of being rejected, the fear of abandonment, the fear of not being good enough. And I know that they were passed on to me from parents who didn't know any better.

The first step toward really living in the present is the daily discipline of being aware of your emotions, of your choices, and asking yourself if you are choosing something from a point of fear or a point of love—real simple. The second step is to follow Emmet Fox's *Seven Day Mental Diet*. (You can order this pamphlet through the

Unity Churches or the Church of Religious Science.) He challenges us not to allow any negative thoughts to control us for a whole week. Not even to allow a negative thought into our minds. Try that for twenty minutes. He says, "and if you can't do it and you're in your third day, you've got to start all over again." Which is clever, because what it's doing is building a pattern in us. The beauty of it is that you're bringing your awareness to it. And that's the point.

My mission statement is to raise one healthy generation.

Creating a healthy generation means that our kids are loved, and we do not get into any kind of negativity that is going to tear the child's spirit down because our own spirit is broken. It means that we realize, and teach, that God is the remedy to fear. It means that we focus on the positive—love—instead of fear and injustices. It means that we clean out pollution in our minds, and become part of the solution rather than the problem.

And so Dad, with his last series, *Us*, was addressing relationships so that we could truly make this the greatest century of all time.

In the acknowledgments page of my first book, I mentioned several people whom I considered real role models. Of course, my dad's huge, but the men and women I listed were all pioneers who saw a purpose in changing the direction of, and created a new, higher standard of living life. They went against all odds, and were truly criticized and hurt, and went through great hardships to make this world a better place. They were strong in character, great in integrity, and they had a dream. They didn't let anyone put them in a box and push them away.

I believe that everybody has the ability to be a hero. The unsung hero was my father's favorite, because he believed that the everyday person was the true hero of this world. He believed that more people should have the courage to speak their truth, to put out more love, to be better people, to be the heroes of their own family.

Be the hero in your life. If you are in a situation where there is confrontation and negativity, be the peace-maker. Yes. Speak up. Do something about it. If you know that a child is being abused, speak up and take a position. If you are part of the abuse, go get help. Be a part of the solution. We can't pretend that it's going to go away, or pretend someone else is going to take care of it. We need to rise to the occasion and to be the unsung hero.

One healthy generation would change everything.

That's all we need: one healthy generation.

# The First Key: Trust In God

I've struggled with my understanding of God. How am I made in His likeness? How is God really the I AM, the I AM who dwells in each of our souls? If He is all-powerful, how is it we are suffering more than we are experiencing peace of mind? Why do the good die first, and the evil thrive? A popular book has been written about the question, "Why do bad things happen to good people?" How is it that our universe is abundant, yet we live in a scarcity mentality in which we can never have enough, no matter how "rich" we are? Questions of this sort, especially when we are in trouble, are cries for help. Where are the answers?

Many people think my dad was a Christian. The truth is, Dad was Jewish, and he hated being pounded by the Christian fundamentalists. He knew that God is love. He didn't believe that one must either give one's life to Jesus Christ or never see Heaven. This supposed "choice," thrust upon Father while he was dying, turned him away from Christian fundamentalism, rather than toward it. He didn't believe in this severe, mandatory entrance requirement to Heaven: "Accept Jesus now or be damned." But, Dad did believe in Jesus Christ as the greatest teacher, often quoted scriptures from Christ in his television shows, and was very respectful of Christ's teachings. So I confirm that Dad really was of "Christ Consciousness." I also believe Dad met Jesus Christ on his way up to Heaven, giving himself to our Lord at that point. I am confident that Dad was appalled by anyone forcing him to believe a certain way. My father dealt with fanatics his entire life, from his insane mother to network executives. So being told *how* he would gain entrance to Heaven repelled him. He complained that severe born-again groups appear righteous by making the rest of us wrong.

In view of the incredible gifts Dad gave to make our world a better place, to think that Dad was unable to go to Heaven because of his belief is wrong.

It has happened to me, too. Even though I am a committed believer in Jesus Christ and attend a Foursquare Church, I have been frowned upon by some fundamentalists because of my links to Gurumaya of Siddha Yoga, Unity Church, and the Church of Religious Science.

I see this happening to thousands of people, and we must come together! To me, it appears very arrogant to think in such limited dogmas, because they separate rather than unite. How are we to get along if we can't accept one another's personal definitions of God? How are we to trust one another and God if we are so busy making the other person wrong? How can we experience global unity in the face of such discrimination? If we don't try to understand and bring out the best in one another, then how can we find the Oneness Jesus promised? This Oneness is the "Christ Consciousness" as a universal family brought together to love one another. God relies on us to take care of one another, not separate and attack each other. How can those of us who follow the Way keep attacking each other, not trusting the other and God?

And how dare we suppose that Jesus Christ is not waiting for all people, regardless of their dogma, upon their ascent into Heaven? I know my personal relationship with Jesus Christ. I just can't understand it when some fundamentalists insist that I don't have an authentic relationship with Christ because I am studying New Thought—a science of the power of the mind to find healing and union with God.

Furthering the confusion, some fundamentalist Christians consider meditation practices learned from Eastern faiths to be evil, even though they are proven by Western doctors and researchers to have valuable health benefits. I practice one form of the Eastern philosophies, Gurumaya's Siddha Yoga, and also find myself in great harmony with the Dalai Lama's philosophies.

We each must come to our own understanding of God, our Divinity, our Higher Power. For myself, I discovered vital universal truths both in the fundamentals of Christianity and in New Thought through *The Course in Miracles*, the Unity movement, and the Church of Religious Science. My ministry studies with Reverend Sue Rubin, my greatest spiritual mentor, combine scriptural definitions from the Holy Bible and research from leading metaphysical teachers of New Thought. Together, that information has led me to explanations to which I could instantly relate, and answered these questions that the fundamentalists do not address.

Since I have been born-again for twenty-five years, certain explanations just didn't make sense enough to me. I am clear about my relationship with Jesus Christ; however, just following a linear, fundamentalist belief system while the chaos continued only offered immense suffering without end.

The "how to trust God" starting point begins with the Holy Bible. Why? My dad often quoted from the Bible in his television scripts. The themes were built upon these scriptures. The next time you see his shows, *Little House on the Prairie* and *Highway to Heaven*, look for the scripture interwoven in his story! So, how do we trust God as a unifier?

Let's agree on the same definition of God.

John 1:1-5, *The Rainbow Study Bible:* "In the beginning was the Word, and the Word was with God, and the Word was God. He was with God in the beginning. Through Him all things were made; and without Him nothing was made that has been made. In Him was life, and that life was the light of men. The light shines in the darkness, but the darkness does not understand it."

John 1:1-5, Holy Bible from the ancient Eastern text: "The Word was in the beginning, and that very Word was with God, and God was that Word. The same was in the beginning with God. Everything came to be by His hand; and without Him not even one thing that was created came to be. The life was in Him, and the life is the light of men. And the same light shines in darkness, and the darkness does not overcome it."

Please tell me, what is the difference? Two extremely different cultures, two different worldviews, yet the same description of God!

*"In the beginning was the WORD."* Our words are sacred. The Apostle Paul said: "Be ye renewed by the renewal of your mind."

Ignorance is darkness, and we control our world with our minds. Therefore, if light is God and God is Truth, then darkness is ignorance, and those who live in chaos, anger, resentment, and resistance are deliberately choosing to live in ignorance's darkness. Perfect love casts out fear. In order to change situations in our lives, we must change our mental attitudes. It is an inside job, working out from within!

*Inner wisdom* is an important key to transform our lives, how we use our thoughts, and the very important daily connection with our Source. The Power Source . . . It doesn't really matter how we make this connection, as long as we make a conscious connection and break through old, limited thought patterns that keep us stuck in persistent, negative thinking. That's what I term, in my seminars, "Playing today's games with yesterdays rules!"

Jesus told us to "love one another," and said, "Perfect love casts out fear." What situations are keeping us fearful? Our society is self-destructing. We're a highly successful technological society, yet we live in a spiritually immature civilization.

Perfect love is the key to living as a unified world. This is simply a shift in consciousness when we remember God as our spiritual source, and we are all connected to this source of light, love, and energy. We are made up of energy. Everything is energy, and energy makes up molecules. Millions and billions of molecules are dancing in synchronicity, reflecting God in action. There aren't these white molecules, separated from the black, separated from the red, separated from the yellow—they dance together!

If you wonder whether God exists, just look up and see the stars shine, the sun rise and set. Feel the heat and cold. What power makes the flowers blossom and winds blow? What generates gravity? It is the same power that breathes life into us, that matures an acorn into a giant oak tree, that speaks in an unspoken language as animals feel our love and fears, and that allows sound waves to vibrate into global communication.

I identify with Dr. Ernest Holmes' description of God as "The First Cause, the Great I AM, the Absolute or Unconditional, the One and Only Spirit or Creative Energy which is the cause of all visible things. Love, Wisdom, Intelligence, Power, Substance, Mind, the Truth which is real, the Principal which is dependable." (*The Science of Mind*, New York: R. M. McBride and Co., 1938)

Once I understood how this Higher Intelligence actually works through us, especially during teeth-rattling situations, my path on the road less traveled changed. My daily practice is to trust in God, and it is a personal journey.

I think we underestimate the value of practicing a simple connection with Higher Mind Intelligence. Whether in prayer on your knees or walking to a meeting, prayer is conscious contact. It doesn't matter how we pray, or where and when, it is personally connecting ourselves with a Higher Power. As long as we deliberately tap into this Higher Power, we can do it at any time. It has nothing to do with one's level of spiritual growth. It helps us as a collective consciousness—that is, if one of us taps in, it helps all of us—to know that God is all-mighty, all-powerful, and all-embracing. For some people, it may be enough simply to acknowledge that they themselves are not God, but rather a reflection of our Lord.

Yet, there is this mistrustful self-righteousness and discrimination circulating within our society, paralyzing us, keeping us from moving onward in synchronicity and acceptance of one another. The current discriminations, resentments, and resistance are not "out there" situations. Rather, healing them is an "inside job." I know we each have a profound capacity to perform way beyond human limits, and there is genius within each of us.

Upon entering my third year as a New Thought student at Westlake Church of Religious Science (while regularly attending the Foursquare Gateway Church with Mom), I discovered a turning point which provided vital truth *beneath and above* the literal lines of the Bible. These classes at Westlake opened grander doors of opportunity to scriptural truths that truly set me free. I offer this liberation to you through these specific seven keys. There are moments in your life which you look back on and remember as turning points. *This is one!*

We are here, at this turning point, because we have been asking the quality questions—the ones that, when answered, will release us onto a higher spiritual path and transform our lives so we may unite as one. Where do we begin?

Make a deliberate choice to take the high road, as a road to our authentic truth, bringing answers to who and how "I AM." These answers lie in our ability to trust in God. The first step is: "Trust in God." My question is: How do we trust ourselves when outside issues are testing us? How are you trusting God? How many times do you second-guess God?

How do we let go of the reins and trust God? I know that as long as God, Jehovah, Jesus, Allah, Alpha and Omega, the I AM, claims "we are created in His image, as I AM" and made in His likeness, then I must start waking up to this soul remembrance. There is a place in you and a place in me where, when we're in that part of ourselves, there is only one of us. Trust God that we are being created in His likeness, the I AM. Whenever we attach "I Am" to our words and thoughts, they become exactly that attraction in our physical world. Stop attaching negative images like "I am tired," "I am too old," "I am not good enough," "I am burnt out," "I am scared." Instead, say, with Tolstoy, "Where Love is, so is God. Where God and Love are, so is Happiness."

We may not be able to predict His actions, control His timing, or wave our hands to create instant miracles. But we also don't need someone to read our tea leaves to tell us our futures. We can simply trust in God, that He is resolving matters in the best, highest, and most loving ways. Use affirmative, conscious thoughts:

> "I am erasing negative patterns and allowing the Higher Power to demonstrate a peaceful and mutually benefiting solution."

> "I am claiming my ability to reveal that which needs to be healed, and heal that which is revealed."

"I am connecting to the Higher Power, and disconnecting to all false sense of negative patterns and beliefs which keeps me from obtaining peace, security, and abundance."

"I am offering to Higher Mind—our Christ Consciousness—all challenged relationships to raise into higher clarity through the Higher Power, providing peaceful resolutions."

I give thanks, as if this conscious contact has been heard. *I let go*, and allow Spirit to work out the details. I detach from the outcome.

Watch out for the potholes and detours, when your mind resists new thought. Say, "I am enthused rather than depressed," "I am blessed rather than cursed."

Attach your "I ams" to "Yes I can." Deliberately vibrate at a higher consciousness. This specifically means raise your physiology—energy levels—with God-filled thoughts. Take the high road, *now*. Make the road less traveled more traveled. Deliberate living is deliberate consciousness.

First and foremost is my foundation in the teachings of Jesus Christ as the God I serve. He is the greatest teacher to me, delivering profound truths that go beyond time. Even if we do not all agree that Jesus is God, we can agree that His teachings are essential truths, as my Dad so believed.

To build an important bridge, I attend a Foursquare Church with my mother, Lynn, who is of the fundamentalist born-again persuasion. My mother is one of my best friends and we have become extremely close since Dad's passing. Though we differ in certain fundamental religious understandings, we share our love and respect for Jesus Christ as God. We differ about why Jesus Christ died for our sins and about his legacy left for us. New Thought metaphysicians believe Our Lord's crucifixion symbolizes victory, overcoming negative attitudes with spiritual authority and the great demonstration of the resurrection principle, taking Christ shedding his blood and dying on the cross for our sins and lifting us up to a new way of living to celebrate life as one universal family.

We are created in the same source. Just as no race is superior, neither is one religion: We are from the same source!

We have an abundance of wisdom from all walks of life. To date, there are the great minds of Dr. Billy Graham, Dr. and Mrs. Martin Luther King Jr., Dr. James Dobson, Rabbi Harold Kushner.

There is the forum founded by Christian motivators, Zig Ziglar and Peter Lowe, and there are the positive thinking ministers, Dr. Norman Vincent Peale and Dr. Robert Schuller.

To explore the science of the mind and the power of deliberate living, we have the work of C. S. Lewis, Andrew

Carnegie, Napoleon Hill, Og Mandino, Harry Palmer, Les Brown, and Anthony Robbins.

At our fingertips is the work of a fountain of mind expanding medical doctors spearheading the Way, including Carl Jung, Wayne Dyer, Deepak Chopra, Jerry Jampolsky and Diane Cironcione, Bernie Siegel, Andrew Weil, and Abraham Maslow. These great pioneers have demonstrated the connection between healing the spiritual mind and the body.

Powerful women such as Mother Theresa, Oprah Winfrey, Dr. Marianne Williamson, and Dr. Clarissa Estes offer breakthroughs about our roots as spiritual women.

The mystics and nineteenth-century New Thought mastery teachers, including Raymond Charles Barker; Emmet Fox; Eric Butterworth; Unity founders, Charles and Myrtle Fillmore; and Dr. Ernest Holmes, founder of the Church of Religious Science, deepen our understanding of the profound "meaning of life" mysteries with exceptional clarity.

The synthesis of all these teachings offers us an all-denominational and universal understanding of God that is in alignment with my teachings. And these teachings are congruent with my dad's philosophies.

I remain in alignment with Dad's wishes to teach "the power of love" on a universal plane to encompass all living human beings. Dad was brilliant with his scripts, touching millions of hearts across the globe with this universal philosophy, because he gave us a road map to unconditional love and believing in a Higher Power without barriers of color, race, and religion. He excelled as both a mastery teacher and a genius in his industry.

## *Remember the First Key: Trust in God*

I declare right here and now that I AM One with the connection to our Higher Intelligence, Infinite Wisdom, and True Love, Our Creator.

I AM,

One Source, One Mind, who is of Us.

I AM erasing all negative and fearful thoughts and emotions taking me off track, separating me from our God I AM.

I AM fully present, aware, and thankful for this divine connection I can tap into at any time. I AM trusting in God right here and right now!

And so it is. Amen!

# The Second Key:
## Choose Love over Fear

"Love, it's what lets us live on. It's the most powerful force in our Universe. Don't ever take it for granted."

—*Michael Landon*

Fear is the great enemy of humankind. It destroys happiness. It imposes limitations. It cuts off positive thinking and reinforces the negative. It blocks the ability of the spirit to use and enjoy the goodness each one of us naturally inherits.

Fear is a primary cause of depression—leading to cancer, our nation's number one killer. Love is the number one key to cure this dis-ease (Oneness is living *with* ease). "It's what lets us live on."

When Michael Landon took me as his daughter, his unconditional love began to overcome my fears. His love grounded in me "living tools" that are rooted in God. How do we go the extra mile, serving our purpose with conviction, sticking to values such as hard, honest work, compassion, and truth between people? How do we hang tough when fear comes knocking?

Perfect love does indeed cast out fear, yet *we* must do the daily work and the weeding. *We* must develop our inner wisdom, *we* must understand how the spiritual principles work in our lives, and *we* must know how to connect with our God, the One Universal Source.

The choice between love and fear always lies in our daily practice. Sometimes this may be a minute-to-minute practice. The good news is that, when we make that simple and deliberate choice, all of God's strength is available to us, and fear melts away!

How we touch other lives is how we live!

How are you touching other lives? Is it with love or fear? Fear has many disguises: from obsessive, controlling actions to ignorant violence.

Fear is the deep core hidden in every issue that challenges us. It is a fact that, in order to heal our fear, we must first return to the times when the errors in our relationships did not exist. For some, that may be in the womb. However, there is always a point in time to go back to. In order to truly heal the wounds we address these errors with neutral respect.

There was public controversy about our family even before Dad's passing. Much of it brought unnecessary suffering, based, as it was, in mistrust and fear. I chose to be responsible for standing up for truth, honoring my father's image as I had promised him. The controversies—including shocking will changes, my brother's movie, and printed and televised documentaries—invaded sacred areas that must remain private, creating more problems. It affected our children, and still does.

Where did the core of our family unit's fear really begin? The core of fear began with my parents' divorce, and therein lies the bridge to reconciliation. Their divorce was public and harsh. Everyone felt the backlash, and it spilled over into all family relationships. I blame the attorneys for creating so much unnecessary pain with their "get it all" and "destroy" attitudes. I remember that Mom, my sister, Les, and I were in Europe when Mom found out all her credit cards had been canceled, with no warning. This seemed so brutal, especially since we were away from home, leaving Mom to resolve the crisis. What a cold-hearted action, leaving us stranded in Europe. This was not the Dad I knew. I know that the attorneys, competing with power and control, must be razor sharp to protect their clients' best interests. But was this really necessary?

Naturally, communication barriers went up, keeping my parents at arm's length. It was shocking to see two people, so passionately in love for nineteen years, become equally passionately angry, leaving the residues of anger running deep into our lives. The publicity was the most damaging. No one in the public eye escapes that harshness, and it left all of us, especially the children, scarred for life.

I understand and respect the courage it took for my brother to present his perspective on Dad in his movie. I know he was not motivated by money to hurt Dad's image or to destroy him, but rather he presented the severe damages of divorce.

Divorce can be nasty! Yet, divorce can be imperative. What we make of it is up to us. We can make divorce a positive transition. We can choose love over fear.

My parents' divorce affected all of us. It affected Dad's business team, and our relationships with them and how they respected us. That was vital in Dad's passing and the will change. This divorce created "sides," and presented negative impressions of us to the public that last to this day.

On the other side, I observed my mom gaining great strength and confidence. She became a loving mother and friend, born again in Jesus Christ. Her strength gave her the courage to be a part of the solution. With other pioneer women who are true visionaries for women's and families' rights, she helped establish a powerful movement called LADIES (Life After Divorce Is Eventually Sane), whose mission is to protect women from cruel divorce settlements. They created solutions, so that women's homes would not be at risk or lost in case of divorce. They developed protocols to address women's ability to generate income after divorce, and to keep ongoing medical insurance for themselves and their children.

LADIES has gotten laws passed, started support groups nationwide, and these courageous women have done all this by donating their time. Turning their lives from fear to love is one example of how these women, who didn't need to do a thing for this cause, genuinely gave of themselves, transforming their own lives into grander purposes for the betterment of the women of America. All of us, and all of our children, are safer because of their selfless work.

Cindy Landon excels as a mother to Jennifer and Sean, and has raised exceptional children, whom I honor as my sister and brother. At a young age, Cindy became the victim of the nastiness of the press. The publicity of the divorce set a precedent with the public, and the press turned against Cindy and Dad. Cindy was called a "blond bimbo," Dad's love for her classified as a "midlife crisis." I simply did not agree with this at all. Dad and Cindy really fell in love, and she is far from being a "blond bimbo." She may have married one of America's very wealthy, most handsome mega-stars, yet she had what it took to capture his heart, mind, and body. I believe Dad had two soul mates, and married them both!

The weeding-out process is how we choose love over fear. Take the time to weed out the core issues and move toward authentic healing. This is the high road. Shun the low road of seeking temporary relief by stuffing your feelings. Weeding out core issues is an ongoing, daily practice—a practice that goes on for the remainder of our lives. The weeding out of our fear-based thoughts impacts all areas of life, in which we are tested time and again until we die. If we don't do the inner weeding of our minds, taking responsibility over our negative patterns, actions, and thoughts, and start building bridges to peace, it doesn't matter who is right and wrong—we will self-destruct.

Our family unit self-destructed because we lost the security of having Dad. Cindy and Dad reacted to the horrible publicity. The publicity affected Mom, and this damaged our family, her family—all of us. The attorneys' demands to get it all—to protect their clients' interests—went way beyond what is needed, into the jugular vein of the family. The divorce war tactics spilled over into our lives, generating fear and hurt. Mom fought lion-fiercely to protect her cubs' den, following the strict guidance of therapists and legal counsel. We were told that Dad was "going through a major change" and that "they don't communicate anymore." The children became the go-betweens, and lost the security of trusting the father and/or mother. This created chaos, and relationships filled with panic and fear.

In any family, such exchanges would ignite an electrical fire, complete with electric shocks lashing out. Who gets hit and, so, badly damaged? The children, who just didn't belong in this fight in the first place. One element was constant in our families: a strong bond of love. Despite our disagreements, there is love rooted in God. I love my family, and Cindy's family, all connected by our love for Dad and his grandchildren. This proves Dad's conviction that the "power of love lives on." Our children motivate me to show up, despite the hurt. The memories of laughter keep the relationships flowing. I love my nieces and nephews, playing with them. I love for my son to visit Sean and Jennifer.

To stop the battles, we came from higher ground and worked out our differences. We made the experience an example of how this power of love lives on, because of the children, and out of respect for the man with whom we all share the major bond—out of our love for Michael Landon.

But how easy it is to get caught up in chaos and fear, the key viruses contaminating our core identities! This happens when we stay stuck in old thought patterns, locked in by old habits. We tend to act on data about who we are with behaviorally coded errors, subconsciously passed down from generation to generation. These need to be weeded out. Searching for viruses is an inside job, and a daily practice.

There is a clear lesson here that I compare to the alchemist who purifies gold. It takes severe, hot temperatures to burn off the dross (that gooey, black junk) in order to get to the pure essence of gold.

I realized that my parents' divorce had resulted in their dross falling on us, and that it was time to separate their past issues from us. We had to allow the gold to shine through us and our children as new beginnings.

For my first action, I needed to go back to both the old business manager—whom I genuinely love and respect—and to Cindy, to seek the truth that would set us free. In the beginning when we attempted to talk, we only exchanged heated conversations with the new business manager—not Dad's manager, but a man who assumed this role after Dad's death. There were family meetings, then each of us went our own way to work out what we needed or wanted to.

For four years, Cindy's children and my son attended the same school, Viewpoint. She and I shared the same school grounds for social events and fund-raising parties, and we were forced together at many other occasions. Yet these meetings, even though forced, were creating stepping-stones towards love and reconciliation. Mr. Arnold Gold, my trusted attorney, came up with a "peace treaty" idea at the same time my ex-husband, Jim, met with Dad's business manager to make sure our son's educational trust was safe. Jim told me to call the manager, and I did. The time was right. I could find resolution by directly facing them, with time behind us to start the healing process.

One phone call changed the direction of my life to a grander, more meaningful relationship! That one phone call broke through the fears and allowed the healing to transform important relationships. How we choose love over fear is how we touch others' lives!

"Love is the most powerful force in our universe. It's what lets us live on. Don't ever take it for granted. Reach out and touch someone's life, daily."

—*Michael Landon*

## *Remember the Second Key: Choose Love over Fear*

The purpose of my life continues to be about revealing more of my divine nature.

I intuitively know, with conviction and confidence, that during conflicts the greater good for my life still awaits my deeper, inner recognition. Even if I am uncertain and fearful, my faith leads me boldly forward to face the uncertainty, fears, and excitement of the greater unknown that awaits me.

I am one with this faith. That means I exercise dominion over my thoughts, feelings, and actions, certain that I sustain conscious awareness of my oneness with the indwelling spirit of God's love and wisdom working in me and through me right here.

I now choose love over fear.

And, so it is. Amen

# The Third Key:
# Believe That Daily
# Miracles Do Occur

When we trust in the Greater Power, our higher intelligence works through us to influence our consciousness and shift our perceptions. That shift—for example, switching from a victim mentality to a victor mentality, or from a negative pattern and attitude to a positive, responsible attitude—is a miracle in itself and it does lead to more daily miracles. Why do I state this with conviction and absolute certainty? The mere fact that we are created in this world is a miracle. We are all miracles. The simple fact that we see colors, hear sounds, feel the wind—just the fact we breathe air is a daily miracle.

I know daily miracles exist. I was given up for dead. I was told I would not be able to bear children. Therefore, I consider my son a major miracle. His life inspires me daily. Yet how many of us take our children's lives and love for granted?

In my own life, the reconciliation that followed the pain and turmoil resulting from my dad's death, and from my own divorce, are indeed miracles.

Let me share the story with you.

Our whole family had been put through emotions, pressure, and scrutiny. We had all lost Michael Landon's physical presence and emotional protection. His life had been the greatest comfort to all of us, no matter what type of relationship we shared with him.

We all loved Michael Landon, and to me he was my "savior." At the same time, I myself was under extreme pressure in my personal life. My marriage was not a healthy one. Jim and I were the best of friends, but not more than that. There was such an uncomfortable tension between us that it was affecting us dramatically! I would find myself crying in my closet so my son wouldn't see me fall apart.

I had lost my savior and mentor, and had no one to talk to who seemed to understand my position. My mom was and is dead set against divorce, and I just couldn't listen any more to how horrible my life would be if I divorced. Dad was gone, our financial security was gone, my home life was falling apart. I would have to develop a career to support my son if I chose to divorce. I had spent all my married years supporting Jim into a very prosperous career, and had forgotten about my own dreams and sense of value. With my burning passion to teach on a global level, I couldn't be just a "housewife." My spirituality conflicted with Jim, who claimed my mission was like "kicking a dead horse in the face."

He is the father to our son, and so dear to the family. Dad loved Jim. I knew this love to be one of great respect for how hard Jim works, how he applies himself no matter how hard the task. Jim's work ethic is the best, and remains so to this day. I know that Jim is loyal, very generous, and extremely good-hearted. But I had my mission, and the chemistry between us was not that of husband and wife. For years, we were on separate paths. Deep within, I knew that to pretend to be in love for the sake of our son was an untruth that would eventually destroy all happiness.

The unexpected blow of Dad's will, coupled with the loss of Dad, took away all my security! Trying therapy with a mate who didn't believe in it proved it was time to part. It wasn't about who is messed up; it was a difference of personalities and beliefs.

How important it is to get to know one another's rules and be in alignment with them before marrying, rather than going into a relationship with blinders thinking you can change the other! Now here I was, having lost my dad, and with a son so very, very dear to us, and no clue how to create a peaceful divorce.

I needed a miracle!

Where do we go to find a miracle? Does a miracle mean making the blind see, and the paralyzed walk? What is the difference between being physically blind and paralyzed, and the traumas leaving us in emotional darkness and paralyzed with fear?

How do we believe daily miracles do exist?

Trust in God, choose love over fear, and believe in a higher power that works through us that we can tap into at any time.

I absolutely would not follow the course of my parents! If anything positive came from their divorce, it was that it taught me never to follow that course! Though there were tough, very emotional months of reorganizing, Jim and I created a peaceful divorce. We used the same attorney. Our son's security, rather than money, was our priority. To this day, Jim and I are the best of friends, and Jim continues to make sure we are protected. I am the most blessed in this transition because we chose love over fear, and stayed focused on the greatest priority, our son's emotional well-being.

Jim married a wonderful woman, Janice, whose two daughters, Shambri and Schyler, are best friends and sisters to my son, and have become goddaughters to me. Janice and I are true Christian sisters, and are working together on projects. When people find out at social events that the ex-husband, wife, and ex-wife sit together, laughing and truly loving each other, they are so blown away! This is a miracle, and miracles do exist because the focus is on centering God, Jesus Christ, in our lives—with our children being the true essence of gold. A golden mind is a golden life!

So, out of what might have been a negative experience—divorce—came positive results. Those results, each one of them, are examples of the daily miracles that happen all around us.

Remember Emmet Fox's challenge in *The Seven Day Mental Diet*, to spend one week "screening" negative thoughts, as we may selectively screen all incoming calls. Truly, you will notice shifts, in the same way that we notice changes in our body when we exercise muscles. We are retraining our mind-thought programming.

Forsaking the negative enables us to count our blessings. Try it. Try to go for one week without allowing one negative thought to dominate your mind.

Try it for one day first. Dr. Fox suggests that first-timers try it for one day, then three days, and proceed to one week straight. I suggest making this practice a priority. This exercise blew me away when I saw how hard it was in daily practice, and how many negative thoughts I allowed into my consciousness. This mental diet is a must. Each of us must use discipline to exercise our minds, controlling the amount of negativity (worry, doubt, resentment) we allow our minds to dwell upon. Once I developed the practice of the Seven Day Mental Diet as a daily habit, the floodgates to Heaven opened!

## *Remember the Third Key:*
### *Believe That Daily Miracles Do Occur*

I claim the presence of God is acting through me right now, directing my thoughts and activities.

I release all opinions about persons and things that impede my demonstration of good. I am released from old thought patterns about what I am not. I move into who I really am.

This recognition allows me to see the same Holy Presence within conflicting relationships; therefore, we become one mind.

I give my full attention to a positive, creative, dynamic idea of God. The spiritual presence within us is directed to find grander ways to appear. I discipline errors of my thinking into positive direction and creative action now!

I am divinely guided and the Mind of God is in action through me. It is now flowing with ease. A greater plan of daily miracles is occurring right here and right now.

And, so it is. Amen.

# The Fourth Key: Take Action Now!

*Take action now* refers to our ability to live in spiritual authority on a daily basis. Whatever path you are walking is no one else's business, but what *is* someone else's business, for example, is how our youth are being affected by violence. We can instantly shift the world's perspective into daily miracles anyone can manifest. We must trust in God, sharing an alignment with God, and each other, to heal our world. Trust in God, but do not remain passive in the face of the challenges in your life and in society around you.

Taking action now means making positive decisions to trust God in every situation, sometimes minute to minute. Errors occur when we lose "conscious contact." Then we act from irresponsible emotions—losing control, yelling, striking back, allowing "bad moods" to control us, perpetually worrying, and suffering panic attacks. Taking action now includes taking deliberate, full responsibility for all our actions, thoughts, and behaviors.

How do we choose love over fear during the times that create resistance, resentment, and chaos? What does it mean "to take action through God during challenging times?"

*Take action now* is how God takes action through us and for us, right here and right now. My work proves to me the absolute perfection of "take action now" through the amazing results of my live programs and shows, "The Highway to Success," "The Highway to Prosperity," and "The Highway to Inner Wisdom." I am in my ninth year of presenting them, and am a proud member of the National Speakers Association. It wasn't too long ago that I was terrified to speak in front of crowds, but I was instantly placed on national television, and confronted with personal questions regarding the changes in Dad's will. Immediately following my Dad's passing, I found myself on enormous stages in front of thousands. There were live shows at the Crystal Cathedral, with Dr. Robert Schuller and his wife, Arvella, delivering both the "International Live Women's Forum" and the televised *Hour of Power*. Together, Dr. and Mrs. Schuller opened doors to "positive living," and a massive shift occurred in my life! Next, I was invited several times to Peter Lowe and Zig Ziglar's powerful Christian seminars, finding myself on the stage set in a forum of ten thousand people.

Delivering live seminars was a major breakthrough, because it forced me to soar out of my comfort zone. When we focus past our barriers, and tap into motivational courage, we allow lasting success. I am constantly sharpening my presentation skills, because my mission is so valuable to me, and picking up the torch was the hardest, yet the most rewarding thing I've ever done.

I have learned from many disappointments and worries, and from taking risks, that determination eventually balances the negative outcomes, bringing outstanding successes and vital growth. One cannot put out positive energy and not get it back—period. It is available simply by rechanneling the creative expression that is the genius within all of us. *Taking action now* amidst challenges creates opportunities to prosper.

Taking action is a creative flow of intelligence. It works as the genius within each of us, and opens us up to this higher intelligence. The impossible becomes possible.

How do we use this higher intelligence? The material I deliver is unique and powerfully effective, because my live shows and radio programs allow each individual to experience the higher intelligence. We create positive results that last, because they come from the same source that inspired my dad to write his shows, touching hearts and souls for us to remember why we are really here. We demonstrate the life patterns and spiritual principles that apply to various challenges in our lives. I tell how I was challenged during the creation of my mission. I use real-life stories.

The "Highway to Success," "Highway to Prosperity," and "Highway to Inner Wisdom" series took years of hard work, fighting home-front battles with the Landon Estate and further battles with my brother and my sister, over his movie and my work. I stayed focused, with intention to serve the higher power, setting a positive course of action. If there is any hope of overcoming life's perpetual dramas, when we feel lost on the "high seas," it lies in how we take action now. I had to let go of my attachment to the battles and focus on the promising, positive course of action.

I want you, the reader, to know there is authentic hope for us. We have major take-action-now people, from all walks of life, deliberately setting forth for freedom from the fear-based, negative, controlling darkness pervading our societies—the worst cancer of all known to humankind. It is this same fear-based darkness that runs rampant, affecting our homes and work.

Daily, I interact with people who are genuinely working hard to save America's youth. I've met presidents and their wives, senators, ambassadors, legendary religious and humanitarian activists, CEOs, educational activists, journalists, radio personalities, and major celebrities, all committed to humanitarian contribution beyond the desire for publicity. This is the inside scoop we need to be hearing about! We need to hear the wonderful stories people are living, every day and night, to offer our youth promises of hope for all humankind. How positive is the news in the news? *Take action now* is about you and me taking back the control we gave up, little by little, because the outlook was so dim.

I am touched by how the everyday person makes this world tick. A movement started by the *Washington Times* newspaper, sparked by a true story, mobilized thousands of working mothers. Some saved babysitting money to donate. All worked tirelessly, donating time and expenses towards the Bridge of Peace ceremonies. This huge, successful movement started in Washington, D.C., commemorating the fiftieth anniversary of the bombing of Pearl Harbor. It is continuing right now, in our schools and challenged areas, transforming those who hate each other into those who can forgive.

This movement is called the Women's Federation for World Peace and Inter-racial Sisterhood Partnership. I have been a member since its inception in Washington, D.C., with George and Barbara Bush. The First Lady served as the grand hostess, and I was so honored to stand next to this *true* "Mother of American Heritage." Coretta Scott King was another keynote speaker with me. Talk about high-powered, genuinely caring, and enormously engaging! Coretta Scott King is also one of my most favorite people! She picked up Dr. King's torch and continues with such passion and power, she has influenced me to continue carrying my dad's torch. We are a part of the quiet revolution taking place as a spiritual movement rooted in authentic love.

Taking positive action further drives home the power. This message lies in all of Michael Landon's television programs, and this "love stuff" is deliberately planted, emphasizing its power during hard times and challenged relationships.

Dad left behind a worthy dream. I had Dad's love and my word I gave to him, and a pledge he left for me—both of us committed to a vision, and to our children. My greatest inspiration continues to be our children's futures.

It is a well-grounded truth that those who dare to build a greater vision for God must risk. Dream, vision, or mission—in every detail of our lives, as we bring God into the center of our dreams, they come true. On this road less traveled, I came upon many sages who showed me that the only answer is to trust in God as my Higher Intelligence. I learned that I would prosper according to how I believe. "Soaring the cutting edge of excellence" is the term I use in my seminars. It is the hardest course of action, yet the most solid ground. It secures a solid foundation. Choices we make affect the quality of our lives and shape our destiny! Sometimes forever.

Our choices affect our perspectives and perceptions. There is always the choice between doing the right thing, or lying as means to gain control and power. How many of us face temptation to act outside of integrity? How many actually *do* act from integrity?

How many people do you know of who act outside of integrity for money? We are judged by a higher intelligence, and it is in His perfect timing. No one "gets away" with *outside of integrity* actions. So, if anyone is ever tempted to act outside of integrity, it is not worth it. Trust God working through us, and become enthusiastic about daily living, knowing a Higher Power is at work.

Once I know there is a grander purpose to every trial, my attitude shifts from victim to victor. I understand that I am attracting these issues into my life. Positive action turns the impossible into the possible, because I challenge my belief system. The greatest breakthrough is to look within and take responsibility for what is creating the error.

The law of attraction is always in constant motion. We are either attracting the most amazing people to take us to the next level, or attracting the most amazing sharks. Taking deliberate, positive action makes room for amazing miracles to occur if we choose love over fear, trust God, and sharpen our skills as enthusiastic individuals—truly involved as a part of a solution, rather than as part of the problem.

Melanie Flamminio is a friend of the family; our sons have known each other since the first grade. Her son is one of my "adopted sons," and best friend to James. I knew her son, Anthony, for years before I actually got to know her. However, we got together every year at my son's birthday parties. We had been sharing visions about broadcasting positive-message radio programs. Melanie and my dad were friends before we met. I had the vision, and needed someone who could intelligently build and organize a two-hour radio show offered by the Wisdom Network, without needing a salary. Mel showed up gloriously! It wasn't until we'd been working together for six months that Mel shared two unusual stories about my dad and her.

One morning, Melanie was horseback riding at Lake Tahoe, on the very trails where *Bonanza* was filmed. She felt my dad's hands grab her and shake her. This was immediately after Dad had made his passing.

"You've got to help my daughter," she heard him say. Melanie thought at the time that it was about Jennifer, the youngest daughter to Cindy and Dad.

The second time was a month after Mel and I were involved with the Wisdom Radio Network. She was making her bed. She once more felt my dad's hands grab her and shake her, reminding her, "You've got to help my daughter." There were several years between these two messages, but now Melanie knew for certain that the daughter was me! Melanie responded to his words and took action—giving me support, direction, and involvement to get "Highway to Inner Wisdom" into action! To date, we have touched thousands of lives with the radio program we have produced. Mel's response to Dad's plea for help for me prompted our success.

How much time do we need to take action? We can start right now—by cleaning out the resentments in our own minds. Resentment clutters up our minds so we cannot possibly see the positive during important transitions, and so we get lost. A good example is road rage. We subconsciously harm ourselves by holding on to grudges when they need to be let go. People become so conditioned to react from hatred, anger, and resentment that it spreads into important areas such as family and other vital relationships, where it just doesn't belong. The most vital action you can take is to put out the raging fires burning within you!

What motivates us to make this attitudinal change? Just look around and see how this negativity is affecting our homes and educational system. Look at our entertainment and media. We've lost control of the "entertainment" which is pumped into our homes—and into our children's minds, hour after hour, night after night. We shrug our shoulders when we read about another corrupt politician, another special interest prevailing, another corporation cheating or deceiving the public. It's time to truly erase all color lines and discrimination, stop protecting the killers and rapists by spending millions on them, and start helping our children by spending these millions on vital educational and life resources to give them positive meaning and direction.

If we are ever to change our world, we must change the motivation in our minds. Stand up and make it happen! Before we can clean up the pollution in the world, we must clean up the pollution in our minds! I know you and I, the everyday people, can stand up and make it happen. There is no time like the present. That's why the Fourth Key to a more fulfilling life is to urge you to take action—*now*!

## *Remember the Fourth Key: Take Action Now!*

There is One Power, One Mind and Intelligence in our Universe and that One Source is God.

I know that I AM One with this, Our Source and Divine Spirit, and filled with God's Spirit.

I AM born of the creative expression of God, and remembering this expression, I trust my guidance from this Source.

As I keep my focus on quieting the mind's worries, resentments, and fears, I begin thanking God for revealing the errors of my thinking and showing me the creative expression for resolutions offering grander purpose. With this new attitude, I know I now demonstrate the Higher Goodness (Godness).

The Higher Goodness is the Higher Creative Expression of God working through me. I can tap into this power at any time.

I am divinely inspired to *take action now*, as God in action.

And so it is. Amen

# The Fifth Key:
## Believe in Truth between People

What exactly is truth between people?

Truth is absolute, and it works on many levels—from the most spiritual to the most mundane. When I say, "believe in truth," I am speaking about the truth as an expression of God, the One Absolute Truth. But of course, we must find truth in every aspect of our lives, even those areas that may, at first, seem far removed from God. Everyone has his or her own truths, including different perspectives and personalities. No one person is exactly like another, so how can we expect another to think exactly as we do? There is no single set of standards, any more than there is only one pattern of fingerprints. Most misunderstandings occur because we expect another person to think and react using the same standards and rules we do. When we criticize someone's personality, we are using our own standards and personal rules. Are wars not created over misunderstandings and trying to change others? Whether

we war at home, at work, or on the highways, wherever—
do we ever bother to go deeper into the truth and understand why others misunderstand us? For that matter, are we
always trying to change others, rather than accepting them?

We each have personal rules we use to determine our
truths with one another and ourselves. Our consciousness
manifests our personal truths as ideas flowing on a
subconscious level, and this is the secret behind our disagreements. When we're "flying on automatic pilot," we
are reacting from subconscious ideas that control our feelings. No one can really know what anyone else is thinking,
or what anyone is really like, except that person.

How many times a day are you aware that from these
subconscious ideas, representing your truths, you are
choosing peace and order rather than chaos and suffering?
Do you find yourself getting sick, frustrated, and feeling
stuck in the same routine? Look within and seek the truth.

How many times a day are you using your personal
rules as truth, expecting to change another, rather than
accepting that they have their own rules as personal
truths, too? It is amazing how we become victims of
others' opinions, allowing them to control our states of
happiness or unhappiness. I often allowed the challenges
in my life, and the opinions of others, to create a state of
happiness and security, or of unhappiness and insecurity.

What have these questions got to do with "truth
between people"? My personal stories in the past nine

years revolve around these introspective "truth" questions. Remember, it is the questions that brought us here, right now. Truth is God's wisdom, and not something we learn in academic classrooms. Neither do many children receive teaching about the power of God's wisdom at home. The American family unit has gone through a major uprooting, and the resulting chaos affects us all. However, out of chaos comes growth.

Here is an example that I witnessed in my own life. My parents' divorce, and the rigid beliefs of some in the family that divorce is a sin, created chaos and unnecessary suffering for all involved. The suffering was so intense that I learned from it, and was able to move through my own divorce differently.

I do not believe it is being truthful to remain in a loveless marriage, to pretend, "for the sake of the kids," or for financial or business purposes. I do believe marriage is sacred. When there are rough times, I believe in seeking counseling, rather than jumping out of the marriage or into affairs. But truth and love go hand in hand, and where there is no longer love, truth cannot thrive. When it came to my own divorce, we tried counseling. Then, after many years, I was on my own, seeking personal counseling because my ex truly believed it was my problem. Any marital challenges involve both individuals. It is never just "your problem" or "my problem." The years spent struggling to change the other are so counterproductive. It destroys so much of the important foundation married couples must build upon.

I deliberately set my focus on our son—that he must be protected and nurtured, whatever the cost. Fortunately, both my ex-husband and I were sustained by this truth, and have been able to resolve the various issues in as loving a way as possible. For the first year, it was very emotional and painful. Yet, the truth allowed Jim to meet his new wife, Janice, and give our son, James Michael, his two wonderful sisters from Janice's prior marriage. To this day, we are the best of friends and I am deeply grateful to Jim for demonstrating consistent integrity. He is the best father to our son, and maintains an ethic of honesty and hard work. He serves as a wonderful family man to his new family, as well as to my son and myself, giving us all the best he can. In fact, we all are giving the best we can to each other. His wife, Janice, and I also work closely together, which provides important security for all our children. Every time we experience upheavals, we bring God into the center, then communicate with each other. It comes from that higher truth between people. The power of this principle, bringing God into the center of our lives, sets us free in every single issue we face on a daily basis. The most important action we take is to bring God into the center of every situation in our own personal quests.

I learned from my parents' divorce: They stopped communicating. We all suffered from this. There was a time when we no longer saw the love that brought them together, and it ended with such resentments. The relationships never needed to take this route, because both my Mom—Lynn—and Cindy, are wonderful women whom Dad deeply loved, though each in different ways. Dad claimed he would never love a woman as he loved my mother, and he didn't. One built him up and helped him build his empire into a mega success; she was his inspiration and best friend, and gave birth to four of his children. The other, he admired for how she excelled as a mother, for her love for animals, and as his new playmate, enjoying their grand lifestyle together.

Both women were soulmates to Dad. He genuinely loved both. Cindy was the last physical connection to Dad's love and us.

As a close observer and confidante to Dad, Cindy offered him another type of soul love, close friendship, adventure, fun, and two beautiful children, Jennifer and Sean. Cindy promised Dad to love each of us, and even named every one of us as her own children to watch over after Dad was to make his passing. She was holding his hand on a video, making this promise and assuring Dad of our protection and continuing his love for us.

This is where the healing remains, because it is her word to Dad that I know he depended upon, from a family member he utterly trusted. This truth remains as a powerful testimony how the truth can set us free or lock us in a gilded cage.

Which brings me to the other issue with Cindy and the Landon estate. The will controversy created such upheaval, and the public fighting between us was hurting our children. I feel the situation requires truth. My relationships with Cindy and her family, including my beloved sisters and brothers, require truth. I am blessed to have had wonderful families to have grown up with, and that remains true to this day. Looking back, our laughter and fun balance out the misunderstandings we shared. I consider us close families, because we always regroup with love as our foundation. My mother is the key to bringing us together in our family times since Dad's passing.

Losing Dad taught me just how precious life really is, and we never know when a life is going to be terminated. The other important factor is our children. Dad believed "love lives on." It is through our children that love lives on.

There is something so powerful about children and their honesty. Our teens are brilliant and bring a variety of fun and lessons into our lives. Dad loved how the older children played with the little ones. Especially during his horrid experiences with the experimental chemotherapy, the children's laughter helped him endure the slow death. Every holiday and weekend with Dad was full of happy memories. The time spent with my Mom and family now is time to put aside our differences and create harmonious moments. Our children make all the difference, for they are pure in spirit and I am very close to my nieces and nephews. We create happy, soulful memories that we will fall back upon during the challenging times. Most of my family has been very supportive. We do have a lot of fun, and I love how the children play with my son, and me, as their proud aunt and cousin. To see my son, James Michael, continue to hang out with his uncle and aunt, and with Sean and Jennifer, continues to show how "love lives on." All of these experiences, the growing pains and rebirths, are the real soul food of how family times nourish the soul!

To allow our differences or misunderstandings to get in our way of loving and laughing together at family functions, to miss out on the children growing up and interacting with one another, is the very destruction eating away at our American roots.

Not everything is rosy in the Landon families. There have been situations since Dad's passing when I was ganged up on over my work. Another conflict has been my very different perspective about Dad than what the public received from my brother's movie about him.

It is not easy being the eldest when one does not have the support of a brother or sister close to one's age. The other siblings who are close in age naturally bond together, and do gang up. Once my husband and I broke up, facing certain situations with certain siblings was awful. I had to get to the core because I wasn't going to change the dynamics of the family, and neither was I willing to sacrifice my and my son's family time and holiday parties. What was it in me that was making me the target, and why was I allowing others' judgments about me to hurt me so deeply, taking away my personal truth and power? How do I rise above feeling ganged up against, and not allow this to have dominion over who I am?

The answer lies within. The targeted person feels a form of rejection, and as long as I was reacting with hurt and anger, our truths would continue to fight each other, rather than resolve themselves if I could simply not allow the attacks to touch me. Bottom line: We are all in this together. We were all reacting with self-righteousness, haughtiness, and arrogant anger. We were all feeling violated and victimized in the misunderstanding. Altogether, whatever misunderstanding was occurring, we were all *misjudging* one another. Regardless of our differences, I remain true to my mission. There are still times when I feel wrongfully ganged up on, but I grow stronger by dwelling with Terry Cole-Whittaker's statement: *"What you think of me is none of my business!"*

This is easy to say, yet quite difficult to really accept when we are so attached to our loved ones. Because I value my siblings, we find ways to mend and work out our differences, while respecting one another's differences. I am very close to my sisters and brothers. In time, no matter what tears us apart, we always make up because our love is authentic. Dad and Mom gave us the best foundation, with many, many happy times that keep us strongly attached to one another.

They gave us a solid sense of family. Dad was adamant about working out differences, instead of holding on to grudges within our families. I love our family times of laughter, "sister lunches," playing with my nieces and nephews, and watching my son play with them. For years, my best date was with my brother Christopher! I discovered so much about myself—about how the ways I reacted could create immense hurt, when I simply could have not reacted. There is great power when we don't react, and instead use deliberate spiritual authority. Rise above and neutralize the emotions, remembering that we are here to cultivate a personal relationship with the Divine Presence, Pure Love. Our roots together create a bond no one can ever destroy, except us.

So many of us are fighting for our truths. We're taught to stand up for them. The current psychological trend is that one doesn't need to put up with another's nonsense—so leave, don't communicate, move on! The spiritual truth remains a timeless truth. As we place judgment and hold grudges towards one another, we create a negative, competitive spirit that depresses love, destroys the spirit, and creates separation rather than unity. How we get back to truth is how we are set free. Returning to truth requires us to go within; clean up our own chaos, resistance, and resentments first. This is how we neutralize, so we don't react with the same level of resentments and resistance.

What is it about your challenge that is feeding the rage? How does that make you personally feel? What is the truth about a challenging situation, from the viewpoint of how you are attracting this lesson into your life, right now?

There are different truths, different sides, and different perspectives. How can we expect to be in alignment with healing our world when we don't know what we truly expect from one another in our own families, at work, in other relationships, perhaps in our own expectations of self? How accepting are we of personality differences? How do we become appreciative of personality differences?

The greatest healing story in my life illumines the answers to these questions. It is the "peace treaty" between Cindy Landon and myself. The last two months when Dad was truly suffering with the cancer, and then the will stuff, had this rippling effect that created mistrust, confusion, and deception. It comes from all sides and continues to this day. Yet, whatever happened back then no longer matters to me. People have their perspective and truth, and the answers died with Dad. I know that there is a higher power, this Creative Intelligence who holds absolute dominion over us. We can choose to ignore this Creative Intelligence or involve it in our lives. Yet, one fact does not change: the existence of this Power.

Whoever made what promises to my dad will be held accountable by this higher power. It is no longer my business to hold anyone accountable. Each person knows what he or she did. What matters to me is the healing relationship with Cindy. This reconciliation with Cindy sets a higher standard for how we can resolve the most misunderstood relationships and conflicts using "truth between people." I may never agree with what was told to us about Dad's will changes, that he intended to leave us, knowing "we'd be very disappointed," without any explanation from him. What matters is that I know in my heart how deeply Dad loved us and was truly concerned about our futures. I know how he did depend upon certain individuals to make sure "we'd never lack for anything." One person has made a difference in these painful events, and that person is Cindy. Her responses to me, even as others try to sabotage us, are truly demonstrations of great integrity and genuine love. Dad trusted her completely, and so do I.

I had to rise above, seek the higher power, go for the truth between Cindy and me. I had to stop the negative press because there had been enough pain. Both Cindy and I chose to start trusting the truth between us, to take the high road, walk hand in hand, and never look back on the controversy.

We are each responsible for our truths and the ideas manifesting either negative or positive actions.

I do place a higher value on my relationship with Cindy, more than being right and more than big bucks, because our "peace treaty" represents our word. Cindy Landon and I exchanged our word, and we are both true to our word. Making our word more valuable than being self-righteous—or "right"—is the starting point to reconciliation and lasting truth between people.

There are times when all we have is our word. Shaking hands represents a bonding agreement to honoring our word. We are created from the Word, and our word is power. Our word must have the faith, discipline, and deliberate authority to make this true. We all stray off track, yet the truth does set us free, and will always continue to do so.

The key to resolving any major difference lies in our ability to stop turning critical eyes on one another. We should, instead, be critical of our own conduct and see that we do control and exercise authority not to make a brother or sister stumble. This means we must resolve our own conflicts *first*, and then take the high road to recognize the enemy as a brother or sister. What I am claiming is a major step *up*, that guarantees positive resolutions!

The truth between people begins with the truth within us. Do you inherently trust yourself and your decisions? Are you weighed down with life's burdens, overwhelmed, stressed out with troubles and unresolved issues in your life? Do you realize how many different sides of truths revolve around you on a daily basis? What does the "truth between people" mean? It means to bridge the gap and accept one another, rather than trying to convert or change each other.

To bridge this gap is to commit to a higher level of consciousness and live from it on a daily basis. As we bring the higher power into our lives, we become centered and focused. This action is like an apple a day. It keeps the doctor away—and the lawyers, too. The rushing, uncontrolled reacting, the emotional dramas we entertain can only keep us in fear and panic. Once we know there is a higher intelligence working through us, connecting us on a definite consciousness level, we stop misusing power, we stop judging, and we know "what you think of me is none of my business." It matters what *I* think about me, taking responsibility for all my thoughts, actions, and practices.

This keeps us from getting sucked into the controlling, rapid waters of the dramatic. It helps us be aware of how we subconsciously react. We can choose to readjust to the disciplined calmness. Do you know why Michael Landon made us cry? So we'd slow down and get in touch with the heart that connects you and me as one. As Dad said so often, remember to not judge one another, and know that no power is greater than the power of love.

Our society was built on challenges, and now great challenges are destroying our youth's future. We can make a difference, and it begins with aligning our personal truths into higher truths. This is what Dad meant by the power of truth between people. This was to have been a great theme in his last series, *Us*. Dad told me how *Us* would be his best work, and that it was to address his concerns about the future of America's next generation.

I believe in truth as absolute power, providing solutions for success on all levels of life, if we can remember our True Self during times of challenge. Imagine, even just as an experiment: We are created in truth, expressing God's Love, made in God's image, and there is God in all of us.

That statement alone has the power of the Word to instantly shift our awareness above and beyond our little challenges and controversies—into the world of miracles. "The truth shall set you free."

### *Remember the Fifth Key: Believe in Truth between People*

The Presence of God is the Presence of One Mind, the Infinite Holy Spirit, that exists everywhere.

I know the Presence of God flows through me, and my focus right now is being directed towards a higher truth, eliminating all resentments, resistances, jealousy, and envy within myself. I ask for the Presence of God to reveal any false judgment within myself, and to heal that which is revealed.

I release all false opinions about the person and situation that distract the demonstration of God's truth.

I am released from all old thought patterns and judgments of what I am not. I no longer attract these people and situations that are not of Good will.

I now give my full attention to a positive, creative expression of God, knowing that God's Presence shines the highest truth and best for all involved.

I give thanks as I lift myself up to One Mind, One God, our Creator in One Truth. "The truth is setting me free."

And so it is. Amen.

# The Sixth Key:
# Build Bridges

John Donne's famous line "No man is an island" has become a cliché, but is no less true for that. None of us can live a fulfilled life in isolation. We are, each of us, part of a family of humankind, and we must take positive action to connect with each other, to help each other, and to improve each other's lives. This is the process of building bridges.

And what destroys bridges? The emotional fires we indulge in, and add fuel to, and pass down to others. The hot sparks of envy, greed, rage, mistrust, lust, and pride become self-loathing. This self-hatred becomes rooted deeply within the memory of our subconscious minds. Millions don't even realize the depths of these entrenched memories. They are twisted around every other memory, and last for a lifetime and beyond—manifesting in the lives of our children and our children's children. The results are fear-based thinking that contributes to our issues with discrimination and prejudice, rage and violence, the separation within humankind. The fires rage out of control, spawning mistrust and manipulation. These fires contribute to our collective consciousness, supporting unethical practices, and controlling our lives. They lead to moral decay, which is eating away, swallowing our future generation. There is no time to pretend this is going away on its own. It is time to wake up and clean house!

That's going to take lots of water. Symbolically, water represents life's flow of everything pure, beginning literally and philosophically in the creative mind that each of us has.

The most powerful demonstration of building bridges in my life happened with Cindy Landon, four years after Dad died. The way we built our bridges and effectively put out the fires is an illustration of how you, too, can wipe out challenges in your relationships, and replace them with peace and harmony.

This transformation between Cindy and myself began when we attended an Anthony Robbins three-day seminar over Memorial Day weekend. The major event was participating in the firewalk. If we could walk through literal fire together, we could walk through anything that life might throw at us in the future!

Anthony Robbins has been touring with his firewalk seminars for fifteen or twenty years, which is amazing, since he is just now only forty years old. Appropriately, it was on Memorial Day weekend that Cindy Landon, her sister, her mom, and I attended his Releasing the Power Within seminar program. This was the first time I had spent three days with Cindy, let alone with her sister, Laurie, and her mom, Marilyn. Anthony Robbins's seminars were also the first time Cindy and I spent valuable time together, working out important differences. As I said earlier, we experienced a powerful connection that I felt was Dad's presence. It was so strong, it took me over at the same time as Cindy. I found myself in tears of joy, telling her how much I genuinely love her; and I remembered the times when we truly had had fun together as family and friends who respected one another. Dad was the step up to this connection, forming a bridge to peace. Anthony's seminars hold a sacred place in my heart. His "Date with Destiny" and "Releasing the Power Within" were major breakthroughs in my life.

As a professional in his field, I consider Anthony Robbins a genius—hard working, committed to results, and the greatest master today in mind control, NLP conditioning, the retraining of our minds. Anthony has greatly influenced my life and remains a special person I love for his devotion, exceptional talents, and big heart. He opened vital doors in my life, and I will always feel a special connection and gratitude!

However, where one door opens, another closes. . . . Where Anthony stops in his conditioning techniques is where I pick up: "releasing the power within" by tapping into the inner wisdom of God authentically! I have a firm belief that, before we can reach "God enlightenment" and Christ consciousness, we must know who "I AM" really is. This is done through Jesus Christ, first and foremost. Regardless of whether you want to accept Jesus as Lord or as teacher, our roots in Christ must be established before we can authentically preach God in seminars, or claim to be a Messenger of God. To learn about other religions is wonderful exposure, yet our true heritage and greatest power is to realize that the authentic "I AM" is to know Christ consciousness first and learn from there.

It is equally important to join both worlds, mind power and God power. It is a fundamental truth that one must be rooted in God first before mastering mind power. To live in the reverse order is treading on dangerous ground; you may begin to believe you are God. My entire life, I've seen wonderfully talented individuals, especially in the celebrity spotlight, take their stardom as evidence that they are greater than or equal to God. In time, they hit bottom hard, and are publicly destroyed or die.

We all have our paths to travel, and it is never too late to wake up and remember our roots, our way back home. We are addressing lasting power, true love, being authentic spiritual beings, and building bridges to world peace. We must use the living tools from both worlds, God power and mind power, in order to grow, succeed, and prosper. You don't need to be a specialist to start building bridges.

Building bridges takes just two people: one to pick up the phone, and another to respond. Involved in this decision to take action and build bridges are millions of ideas, thoughts, and beliefs, some dancing like stars in the sky, and some colliding like asteroids into one another, swallowing us into a black hole of emotional darkness. The dark times create a fear that there is no way out. We take on a victim consciousness, and feel righteous about feeling victimized. But if we can step out of that, and choose to build bridges, challenging circumstances offer us the most powerful opportunities to manifest a grander plan.

Just imagine for a moment, what if this "black hole" is really a sophisticated force, so powerful it leads us into another dimension of time and advanced growth? Would we be more open-minded to this challenge, and allow the creative expression to move us toward a rebirth? It has been proven that energy and mass are fundamentally interchangeable. Similarly, both our negative and positive thoughts and ideas are energy, waiting for mind to direct their course. What does this have to do with building bridges? Everything.

The universe is made up of stars, planets, those mysterious black holes, great powerful empty spaces, and the sun as our most powerful energy force. They all run in a pattern ordained by a higher power. How can we not be a part of this energy force? Since the whole universe operates strictly on *love*, why can't humankind?

Love is energy, and energy goes on forever.

Whatever is keeping you from building bridges, whatever is allowing hot fires to control your life, look within and see how those negative thoughts are charges attracting more and more like-minded fires. We can choose to not live in envy, greed, jealousy, pride, lust, rage—which are all based in fear.

Love is the key, and I'm not talking about some sentimental, trite use of the word love, nor do I mean some "woo-woo" weirdness.

It is both scientifically and spiritually proven that love is *energy*, and this energy is God as the absolute power, the driving force.

We are created in this force called love, and have access to this power at any time. This power never changes. It is always here. My near-death experience definitely was, and remains, a most powerful transformation and witnessing of this higher energy force. My dad witnessed this power immediately, and made his promise based on this supreme, authentic higher power at work through me, dramatically transforming Dad and affecting all his television shows thereafter.

Tragedies affect each of us differently. It took a long time for me to understand the impact of the supernatural experiences. I set sail into those oceans which I'd not yet explored, but that had been explored by great, masterful spiritual minds. I did experience an energy force, a wisdom, and shared conversations with Jesus Christ. I am aware of a very intimate, higher power and presence I claim as God.

I remain human, and vulnerable to the daily fears. But my awareness stops the negativity from controlling me. How many of us feel envy, jealousy, pride, greed, rage, fear? If we are not aware of them, these dark emotions can control our thoughts, and these thoughts release a vibration affecting all those around us.

Love is also within us. As we cultivate love within, so it shines outwardly. Fact: If there is conflict in the subconscious, mind will have its way.

We have choices: light and love, or dark and fear. Stephen Hawking writes about the black hole having extremely powerful, sophisticated energy that would swallow everything that would give its presence away. This is a wonderful metaphor: We *do* have the power! It is *around* us, *within* us, and *is* us, as we are of this power. We are like an ocean, millions of drops together, related to one another.

We must deliberately release the negativity that binds us to the harmful and self-loathing ways that we are passing down to our youth. We can take light and God's wisdom to the black hole. As we thirst for water, so we thirst for the extremely powerful and sophisticated energy—of love.

No man is an island. The water sustaining my inner being is God's wisdom. I built bridges. The higher intelligence guided me as clearly as with a road map to the high road, a road less traveled. Any time we choose the high road, and ignore the low road of revenge, anger, hatred, we are making a connection—building a bridge—which will enable love to travel in both directions. This is positive love in action, having dominion over our thoughts, and taking control with spiritual authority. This power guarantees outstanding results that last as long as we practice.

I also know the truth about you and me, about why we are here. It is up to each one of us. Here is the truth that we can start with and with which we can put out those raging fires within us. I was told after my car crash that God must have a special purpose for me. I was a chosen one, a miracle. I've traveled on the high road for twenty-five years. I was blessed to be formally educated in the fields of education and curative psychodrama, and I did graduate work in special education. A professional teaching career followed—the hardest of struggles, yet the greatest of rewards. After that came nine years of professional live shows sharing these teachings. After all this, and two years on radio and three in ministry, I now know this: God has a special purpose for each of us, and there is a creative genius in each and every one of us. *We are all* chosen ones, and miracles. We are born in God's creation and perfect love as miracles. I believe we are here to "love one another."

Like my father before me, I am carrying the torch to remind us about this power of love to build our bridges to God and to one another. My radio experts address a common question, "Is life fair?" Dr. Bernie Siegel best answers this question: "Life is not so much unfair as it is difficult. Ahead of us lies difficulty, and to live is to suffer; but to survive is to find meaning. It is finding this meaning that gives purpose, and the choices we make create meaning in our lives."

Once we learn that life's obstacles offer us outstanding opportunities to grow, creatively replacing the suffering with special meaning, we move on and up in our lives with a grander purpose. The most important bridge we can build is first within ourselves. Our daily focus must be to put out the raging fires in our minds, to weed out the ideas and thoughts that sabotage our ability to love, and to quit blaming others for our challenges, regardless of how justified we may feel. This is an awakening!

What a powerful awakening, the moment I realized that, in building these bridges to other people, I was also building my own bridge to God! God's love is a connection which occurs within us, working through us and for us. Having made this conscious connection, I feel this higher power and intelligence. It surrounds me—all of us—daily.

## *Remember the Sixth Key: Build Bridges*

I recognize there is One Mind, One Presence emanating creative expression and higher inspiration revealing Itself to me at all times. This Presence is God. I am aware of this creative expression inspiring me to release negative ideas formed from desperation, and of all false truths manifesting as destructive relationships, keeping me from connecting to our higher intelligence right now and right here. I tell subconscious mind to take every negative idea, destructive thought, and get it out.

When my relationships seem challenging, I replace fear and anger with higher truths about myself.

I form a divine connection with God and build bridges for our highest best.

And so it is. Amen.

# The Seventh Key:
## Don't Judge Each Other

O n the night Dad informed us he had three weeks to
live, my world crumbled. He said to me, "I'll always
be with you. I'll find a way." Three weeks later, on July 1st,
1991, he made his transition. The next night, strange signs
occurred. First, I had vivid dreams of Dad talking to me
about the will, and that he was upset over the monies. My
bedside lamp turned itself on, so I knew I was awake and
not dreaming. For the next three nights in a row, the
dreams continued and the lamp turned on in the middle
of the night. At first I wondered if I had been subconsciously turning it on, perhaps in my troubled sleep. But by
the second and third nights, I knew this wasn't true. There
was a higher force in action.

I had no idea at that time why Dad was appearing to
me, seeming to be so upset over the will. But I soon
understood. After the will was read, we all realized that
changes had been made, without Dad telling us about
them, or why they were made. The business manager left

us with these hurtful words, "He knew you'd all be very disappointed. But you know how your father gets once he makes up his mind. I tried my very best to persuade him." This pivotal moment when my assumptions about security for myself and my son were shattered left a scar. It gave rise to the questions that began my personal journey of overcoming. And these are the questions that have brought us here together, across the pages of this book.

The Hereafter does exist! I was completely convinced of that when Dad kept appearing to me, and the bedside light kept turning on and off. There have been many more such experiences. The most profound demonstration I've ever witnessed that love is eternal, and that our loved ones remain with us, is told in part 3, The Rose and the Fountain. This was truly one of the most important experiences in my life, demonstrating the power of love that can reach across the barrier we call death. Such a power reminds us that "there is something of a royal lineage, sacred ancestry, and divine heritage buried in the depth of our being. It yearns for us as much as we yearn for it. At some moment in our lives, we reach a point when it calls out to us, 'set me free!' This is the call from our passionate soul, which has been desperately trying to get our attention our whole life, but we have been asleep." From a sermon, "The Royal Self: Living Successfully," by Reverend David Leonard, Unity Church. This is a soul remembrance that brings us full circle, and returns us home. We are born again.

How easy is it to get caught up in our trappings, comfort zones, in old belief patterns that don't serve us. These things force us to hide behind our masks, worn for security because we fear showing our true selves. Slowly, as we cling tightly to these limitations, we eventually form a personal cage. We create it as protection, but it becomes a prison. Judgments are the limitations acting as the very cages that lock us into prison. What if we step out of our cages? What if we dare to soar the cutting edge outside of our comfort zones? Our perceptions start to shift and expand. We are definitely out of our comfort zone, and that can be scary. It also is extremely liberating!

Nine years ago, I was forced to let go of the familiar security factors in my life. I set sail on the high seas. Everything in my life was an unknown, and I was challenged in all aspects of survival. To this day, and probably forever, I am sailing on these high seas, out of my comfort zone. Every day, in every way, I am forced to wake up and look at things in my life differently, using deliberate spiritual authority.

It is clear that we are human, and in being human there is so much of our own "stuff" to clean out and make new. To go around judging others, using yesterday's rules for today's games, takes the attention off our own growth. We become locked in these cages. The shifts in our perceptions are the daily miracles we each can make, and must make if we are to grow into a responsible, mature civilization. Doom and gloom is only in our minds, and we can erase it at any time! The miracle is in cleaning up our own lives and aligning ourselves with the Higher Power. It doesn't matter how people believe in God, or for that matter *if* they believe in God. God *is*—always will be, and always has been. God is constant, formless energy, and is always here for us.

If we are to offer a world of peace and prosperity to our young people, if we are to see profit result from integrity in our corporations, if we are to truly serve our people by pursuing the American dream in politics, we must take the high road. If we are to provide a flourishing educational system so all can achieve their dreams and work toward authentic peace within our nations and civilizations, we must clean up the "errors within" by cleaning up our own relationships, beginning with self.

For myself, to clean up those experiences using the "high road" meant correcting the errors of my thinking. Each one of us can immediately demonstrate positive, authentic shifts away from the negative, persistent patterns that affect emotions, attitudes, and behaviors. The key word is "authentic." It is the real stuff, and is everlasting, ongoing work we must do on a daily basis. This is the road less traveled, and returns us to our natural essence of who we are, rather than the daily search for "who am I?" This creates a stability that grounds us to a solid source so that we do not live off others' opinions, limitations, and goals for us.

I believe judgments are personal, and can be as destructive as they are constructive. The greatest judgment we make is that of ourselves. Yet, how easily we allow others to determine who we are, and affect our self-image and our dreams.

An illustration of this is how my dad, after thirty years of success with his television series, still faced severe criticism among the network executives when he proposed *Highway to Heaven*. Dad was living in Malibu with Cindy. One network executive sarcastically responded to Dad, "Who do you think you are? The Jesus of Malibu?" Dad responded, "Get it right, I am Jewish. Call me the Moses of Malibu." Dad had a powerful tool to transform the critics of the world. He had the most amazing sense of humor! He was one of the wittiest, funniest, and most playful individuals I've ever known. His sense of humor provided us with vital tools to step out of our own emotions and take the high road. He taught us to view each jarring situation, each individual challenging us, even ourselves, from a higher perspective.

Compassion is another strong emotion that allows us to unify, rather than separate. Compassion is a tool for transformation that Dad passed down to me and to the world through his shows. Compassion goes beyond sympathy, and into empathy. It grows into a soulful heart-to-heart unification. We become considerate of others, and demonstrate love for one another.

Michael Landon was one of the most compassionate human beings I've ever known. He was charitable, generous, and determined. His compassion constantly pushed him beyond his limitations and out of his comfort zone in service to others.

He was a man who constantly endured others judging him. It began when he was one of only two Jewish kids in the neighborhood. The prejudice continued in various forms. He lost his dream of an Olympic javelin scholarship that he thought would bring freedom because the football players hated and tortured him as a Jew with long hair. He lived through the scandals of divorce. He knew all about being judged.

Not judging is a lifetime journey. Taking personal responsibility for all our miscommunications without manipulating is true power for forgiveness, allowing love to flow. It is amazing how little we use the God-given genius we are all born with.

As a boy, Michael Landon never knew the love of a nurturing mother or had a positive parental role model. He didn't have a place to go to when in grief or confusion. He did, however, have an old broken-down car that wouldn't even run. Once, he told me, "I could dream of being whatever I wanted to be in that car. I could escape the violence going on in my home."

Michael Landon missed the comfort of growing up in a God-loving home. He was enormously inspired when he met my mom, and together they realized super-star dreams. Dreams do come true. The more Dad became famous, the more he touched lives with genuine love. He knew the value of "don't judge each other" through his own personal pain, his challenging experiences, and his relationships. Dad loved his wives, and all the children. He claimed that his crew and closest friends (Susie and Kent McCray, and the Flinns) were family. He proclaimed on *Good Morning America* that he had the "best life, the best wife, great kids. Soon the world will be a better place because of my kids. They're good people." To me, this is universal as well as personal. He meant that love lives on—through our children. Soon the world will be a better place, because we have all we need right now in our "life tool box" to set us free and out of the cages . . .

All it takes is the willingness to step out in faith. Say, "Show me the faith," and it is here, right now. The faith that is needed is an inclusive faith, not an exclusive set of beliefs. It is my dream, and Michael Landon's, to bring people together, uniting in God as a family. We must let go of pushing our particular religious dogmas on each other, saying to each other what some said to him, "No ticket to Paradise for you!"

How we pray is very personal. It is a conscious contact with the Higher Intelligence that we have at our fingertips by tapping into this greater power—at any time, in any way, in all situations. There are no operators to go through, no chance of being disconnected, no struggling with busy signals that keep us stuck. Neither do we need directory assistance—and it's free!

I told you before that it is the questions that brought us here. The answer lies in these questions. How is it that this man, who had every right to be angry at the world, taught us about the power of love? How did he become so grounded in his belief that God exists as truth between people, that we are made in God's image, that there is God in all of us?

Why is it that Michael Landon tells us so strongly, "Stop judging one another"?

Simply because judgment is the path to misery. I found that out myself before I turned toward love and forgiveness. To paraphrase Ernest Holmes, one truth about judgment is that the Universe holds nothing against us except our reaction.

Michael Landon serves as a wonderful example of transforming tragedies into super success opportunities. He was genuine and honorable. He deserves a positive memory, as an authentic individual who made a dynamic, inspirational difference in our lives, bettering our world. Yet he was also very human. And it is in our humanness that we have our differences.

We will have differences the rest of our lives because of our different personalities. Yet we share one common factor, our creation from the One Source. That Source is the Consciousness of God, and we are one with the loving Presence of God who has left His perfect imprint upon our souls.

Let's take our differences, and choose unity, rather than creating chaotic fears that take us deeper into the darkness of being lost. We become so absorbed in losses and injustices. We get lost and start to judge every single event. Thoughts drive us into a narrow-minded, single direction that sets off sparks and fires. Our narrow-mindedness sets off raging fires inside, manifesting outside. For example, road rage—"That S.O.B. cut me off on purpose."

But that "S.O.B." may well be consumed with vital project plans, and not paying attention to the traffic, unintentionally cutting you off. Yet, how we judge one incident can set up our whole day, attracting one negative experience or person after another. We get so lost in the drama, judging with passion or rage like the god Zeus, who misguidedly throws his thunderbolts.

We truly make a dynamic difference simply by choice. We can choose to align to a higher truth. Doing so grows our consciousness, which automatically brings healing to our relationships. We find ourselves living authentic lives of love.

What Jesus taught about judgment applies to all of us, regardless of who we believe he is.

"Don't judge each other" means taking personal responsibility. If you cheated someone, hurt, violated, manipulated someone, you have time to clean it up. If you feel injured, weed out the injury with God's help.

Anyone with common sense knows this key is not about hatred, or getting revenge. We are all tempted to get quick results and show our enemy who has the power. But we can choose to be governed by a higher power, our Creator.

This key is about living in deliberate, spiritual authority. Taking care of personal business:

- Take personal responsibility to pull up the weeds in your own backyard.

- Every day, bring awareness to your cobwebs, fears, and negative persistent thoughts and behaviors.

- Make the time to connect with God *daily* and clean out the pollution in your mind. ("To reveal that which needs to be healed, and to heal that which is revealed.")

- Upgrade your seating to first class, taking challenges. With truth, seek that which is honestly keeping you from experiencing the more meaningful relationships and abundance of wealth that truly give peace of mind.

- Remember that there is a timeless Higher Intelligence, and greater power of love that creates us.

- Remember that each of us has our source and center in God.

"Judge not lest ye be judged, " means to me that whatever the challenging experience, no matter how victimized I may feel, I *must* go within myself to find out what is attracting this in my life. I must empower myself with truth and faith. I must acknowledge the power that my emotions have over my state of being, for my true power comes from the Higher Intelligence. Therefore, I must suspend my anger, and "turn the other cheek." I have the power to choose a different attitude, to not react from emotions, to not rush to judgment.

"Don't judge one another" recognizes the power in "Who I am."

This is our higher self. This higher self does not respond to anger with vengeful thoughts, or by continuing the victim game, however righteous. To do this keeps us in prison and away from living meaningful lives!

We know the world is full of tragedy. We know there are children at high risk. We know people cheat, lie, manipulate, deceive, and violate. Our world is in a dark state of consciousness. The miracle is you and me; we are the chosen ones. I am challenging us to demand a greater purpose, higher standards, to take action now to be a part of the solution, not the problem. Take personal responsibility through trust in God.

If we are truly judged by our own acts, and by our own acts alone, and if we trust there is truly a higher power at the command center, then punishment and reward are automatic. It does not require my judgment or yours to execute them.

As we focus on fear, we attract fear. Focus on love, and doors open to a greater, more expansive, enormously engaging life of opportunity.

Tell me, who is perfect? Who has nothing to work on? My dad spoke about his own imperfections publicly. In my deepest heart, I think my dad died from the stress of fighting the worldly demons. I watched him give unconditionally, offering unrelenting, incredible acts of generosity against all odds for thirty years! He was a genius, and never got the respect from his industry that he deserved. If the business manager made a promise to my dad to watch over us, then I must allow the cosmos chips to fall as they fall. I've intentionally kept my son's precious educational trust in this man's management, believing that we are coming together with the love, honesty, and faith Dad had in us to work together, to bring out the best in one another. I have loved and trusted this man for thirty years. I want to remain with this trusting love today.

There is no finger-pointing. It is about taking personal responsibility over every area of our communications. Whether we experience miscommunications or perceive another's opinion in a different context, it is our personal responsibility to build bridges, knowing there is a greater power, a higher force that is in command.

As Jesus said: "As you sow, so shall you reap." I think that's a fine principle by which to live our lives.

How do we stop judging, stop blaming, and stop *feeling* victimized, even if we really *are* victimized?

Actually, the answer lies within each one of us. The answer is in the belief inside of us that is actually attracting this situation into our lives. As we believe inside, we manifest on the outside. Recognizing this powerful law opened up my cage and set me free. It gives me the confidence to step out of the cage and explore the lands in our vast universe. Taking personal responsibility by looking within forces every one of us to open up our cages.

The only one who can discover the meaning of your life is you. It is a personal journey. And a powerful key is to live without judgments.

The only judgment that matters is our "final judgment"—regardless if one believes or not. God's presence is just like the air we breathe. You don't see the air, but you absolutely know it is there. Believe it or not. The final judgment exists day by day, and we're not talking about the new millennium, or the End Times.

## Remember the Seventh Key:
## Don't Judge Each Other

*The 1981 Hollywood Christmas Parade was Michael Landon's last parade appearance. He told his fans along the route: "Remember guys, don't judge each other!"*

I align myself with higher self, my higher intelligence, requesting God to reveal that which needs to be healed, and to heal that which is revealed.

Through the power of discernment, God reveals what I am mastering and separates out false judgment that I still need to confront and learn from. I am thankful for this opportunity to learn and master, using God to reveal and heal.

I am opening up more to my ability to tap into higher self—higher intelligence, God as my creator—at any time. I recognize my connection with love, revealing truth I can trust.

And so it is. Amen.

# Part Three:
# The Rose and the Fountain

When my dad found out he had three weeks to live, he established some rules. And one was, "Don't cry," because it was too hard on him emotionally. But when we were saying goodbye that night, I was alone with my father and I broke down and I started crying in his arms and I said, "Dad, I don't know what I'm going to do without you. You're my everything, you're my savior, my best friend."

And he started crying and he said, "I will find a way to be with you. I will always be with you."

But then, after Dad made his passing, we found out that we had lost the majority of our inheritance, that there was no security in our lives or for our children, and that Dad hadn't left anything in writing. He left no explanation for why he did it. The business manager callously told us, "Your dad didn't want you kids to be lazy. He was appalled by the fifty percent taxes in the estate, and he wanted the grand lifestyle for Cindy and her two kids." This was all we knew. It was just a bitter, hurting, horrible feeling.

I knew that if I were to attack Cindy and the estate, I would be attacking her children and I would be attacking my son and the future generation. And this was not what love is about. But choosing love over fear was a daily challenge. It wasn't easy. My hair was falling out. I had blisters on my body. I had hives breaking out because I was so angry. The high road didn't get results immediately. It didn't bring financial security. But I had to release the hatred inside me, because it was taking me down. Not her, not them, but me.

These people who I thought had taken our money—inside them too, is God. I had to find that in them, rather than seek revenge. I needed to reach out and find a way toward positive reconciliation.

It took a long time.

I had to get more into the studies, more into living the truth, more into taking the high road and finding positive solutions. I had to learn to better live what I preached in my seminars. They do say that what we need to learn the most is what we teach.

My dad had told us to love one another. But I needed a demonstration from him. I needed to know that he was there. I didn't want to feel like I was totally out there on my own against the world, against some powerful people who had all the money. A couple of the estate people had attacked me publicly. My dog had been poisoned, and I had found obscenities written on the walls of my house. I felt very alone.

So, I said to my dad one day, "If I'm going to take this high road, and keep this promise that I made to you, you've got to show up for me. Because otherwise, I'm not going to bother."

He knew I was terrified to do television shows without him. And it was there in my room, during the day, I heard very clearly my father saying in my mind, "I'm going to leave you a long-stemmed red rose before you do your first big show."

I was supposed to do the Geraldo show, and Geraldo had found out about the will and he was going to use it on television. And I was thinking, "Geraldo is just—he's a shark."

So I was in New York City, in the Hilton Hotel, and I happened to take my friend Carolyn on that trip with me. And I heard Dad again, during the day, very clearly in my mind, "Cheryl, I want you to go to the fountain in Central Park."

Well, I didn't know Central Park. I'd never been to Central Park. Who sends their daughter into Central Park in New York City, without a clue where some fountain is? But I told Carolyn and she said we had to go. It was about a two-mile walk, maybe longer, but the interesting thing is, I never skipped a beat. I never got lost. It was as though a higher power was guiding me.

We were so fast, and going up and around, and into these areas and slopes—it was just a maze. I came to the top of this stairwell, and there was a fountain, but there was nobody around this fountain.

The area was empty. So I walked down the stairwell, and right exactly where I stopped, there was a long-stemmed red rose. Right at my feet. Carolyn nudged me and said, "Oh, my goodness, Cheryl, look up." We were at the fountain of Michael the archangel.

My dad had found a way to demonstrate the power of love.

The show went fine. Not only did it go well, but I told Geraldo up front, "Do not talk about the will. This is about the mission." And he didn't. He was wonderful. He even came up on stage and held my hand to assure me that everything was okay.

So that is the story: love is energy, and energy lives on. Love is the most powerful force in our universe. When we choose love over fear, we choose the most powerful force in our universe. When we come from love, we're coming from the most powerful force in our universe.

I think of God as an ocean, and of us as a drop in this ocean. We're all connected. This isn't about one right religion. It's about connecting with the highest power, on a daily basis, moment to moment.

Our kids are depending on us. These kids are having sex prematurely and are having babies in order to try to gain acceptance. They are using guns as a reflection of the hatred, the anger, the fear that we're passing down. They need to learn that there is another way. We all need to become clear about who we are, so that we understand that we are here to build a greater world together. And there's nothing to fear. Fear will not exist.

# The Power of Love

Michael Landon said, "I most deeply believe in God, I believe in family, I believe in truth between people, I believe in the power of love. I believe that we really are created in God's image, that there is God in all of us." In *Highway to Heaven*, he referred to God's power as the "stuff," The Power, The Source! I think of him as a heavenly angel, still very much alive. I miss his hugs, laughter, and guidance, but I know he is with me. Michael Landon's love for us and for God withstood immense pressure and ridicule. Acting from his conviction and good-heartedness, against all odds, he used global television to teach us about the power of love. He truly tried to make this world a better place, and I believe he is still working to do that. We can continue to keep Michael Landon's legacy of love alive. It is a universal legacy, which reaches far beyond the fame of one man. It is a plea to "let there be peace on Earth—and let peace begin with me." Each of us must make conscious choices to let love and forgiveness into our lives, especially during those challenging times, and live in deliberate, spiritual authority—this is the road we must travel to guarantee the safety of our future generation.

In his final days, Michael Landon said, "Live each day as if it were your last. You never know when it is going to be taken away." To me that means living each day to its fullest, building bridges, using the high road. It means transforming the road less traveled into the road more traveled. Join me on the Super Highway. And, don't judge one another . . .

Go with God!

Namaste!

I invite you to join me on this high road. Please visit my website at www.cheryllandon.com. There you will see regular updates about our radio topics, live seminars, upcoming books, teaching stories, and about the movie that will be made based on this book. You will find out how you can become involved with our various peace movements and programs that keep Dad's and other humanitarian activists' positive work alive, to make the world a better place for our children.